TEEN
VIOLENCE
IN AMERICA

TEEN
VIOLENCE
IN AMERICA

JOSEPH KOLB

Hatherleigh Press is committed to preserving and protecting the natural resources of the earth. Environmentally responsible and sustainable practices are embraced within the company's mission statement.

Visit us at www.hatherleighpress.com and register online for free offers, discounts, special events, and more.

TEEN VIOLENCE IN AMERICA: HOW DO WE SAVE OUR CHILDREN?

Library of Congress Cataloging-in-Publication Data is available upon request.
ISBN: 978-1-57826-811-5

COVER AND INTERIOR DESIGN BY CAROLYN KASPER

Printed in the United States
10 9 8 7 6 5 4 3 2 1

CONTENTS

INTRODUCTION

AS A VETERAN crime reporter, I was accustomed to violent crime scenes—not only in the U.S. but from my time spent on assignment in Ciudad Juarez, Mexico and San Salvador, El Salvador, two of the most violent non-combat cities in the world. It was my job to paint a written picture of the incident, including its causes, potential impact, and outcome. In this position, I spoke to many family members who were forced to identify loved ones—victims of oftentimes grisly deaths.

In all my experience, it was always the cases involving young perpetrators that left me truly bewildered. As my journalistic career eventually gave way to a career in criminology and corrections, I sought to understand and ultimately counteract the reasons why people, especially young people, senselessly hurt each other. I struggled to find the logic behind why a seventeen-year-old would stab his girlfriend to death just because she broke up with him; or why a sixteen-year-old would shoot up his school because some of his classmates made fun of him. These are compelling, important questions, which when left unanswered can haunt communities for years and years.

For our purposes, it would be best to distinguish between *criminal juvenile behavior* and *juvenile delinquency*. Oftentimes, the two terms are used interchangeably, resulting in the lines between them becoming blurred.

Criminal juvenile behavior refers specifically to those instances involving more serious crimes such as burglary, armed robbery, battery, and homicide. These events, once thought to be rare anomalies, are now occurring with regular frequency.

Juvenile delinquency, by comparison, is relatively benign—albeit still disturbing and a potential stepping stone to criminal behavior if left unchecked. It is also by no means a new phenomenon; quite the contrary—youths have been testing the boundaries of parental and societal rules since the beginning of time. Oftentimes, these acts of rebellion don't result in any physical harm—acts of vandalism such as throwing a rock through a window or spray painting a name on a wall appear harmless—but they still involve a victim. The owner whose property has been vandalized still incurs the cost of clean-up and repairs, as well as the personal violation of space and property. When minor crimes and public mischief goes unanswered or is ignored, the potential for serious crime increases (in what is called the Broken Windows Theory, discussed in Chapter 12).

In April 2018, we had multiple incidents in a southeast Albuquerque neighborhood where groups of teens were stomping on and breaking the windshields of vehicles parked in the street. Alyssa Gonzalez, one of the victims' mother, was angered that her son's windshield had been broken for no reason. "He just got this car a couple months ago from his grandpa, and he's been working really hard and getting it fixed up and looking good," she told a local television station. "He put his time and effort into it just for other kids to come and destroy it, so it's frustrating for him".[1]

Gonzales expressed her anger and frustration not just at the culprits but also at their parents. "I think we need to support our teens more and, honestly, parent better."

In December 2017, a sixteen-year-old girl in San Juan County, NM was so intoxicated that her mother called sheriff deputies. When they arrived, she was found lying in the street. A neighbor told police the girl was previously holding a shotgun, which he had since secured. The San Juan County deputy was putting the girl in the back of his vehicle when she became increasingly belligerent, kicking out a window and stole the vehicle, ultimately crashing into three cars causing it to stop.[2]

Perhaps the most famous juvenile delinquent is George Herman "Babe" Ruth who, at seven years old, was placed in St. Mary's Industrial School for Boys in Baltimore, Maryland. Ruth was a handful for his parents, who had no patience for young George's proclivity towards tormenting local police and residents alike with his words and actions, as well as his habit of overindulging (a habit which he would carry with him into adulthood). St. Mary's was formally an orphanage but was also known for dealing with "incorrigible" children, making it more like a reform school—with strict discipline meted out in the form of corporal punishment. It provided the sort of structure that children like Ruth subconsciously hunger for.

The rest, in Babe Ruth's case, is history. But for other St. Mary's alumni such as Joseph Haines, his admission to the school came as the result of a violent crime. In 1904, a drunken eleven-year-old Haines accidentally fatally shot his friend, Thomas Gordon, age seventeen.[3]

Fast forward a century later, Robert Emmet Mara, an advocate for the rights and safety of children in Baltimore, still sees many of the same obstacles Ruth and Haines were confronted with as very much present in turn of the century Maryland. He advocates for more structured environments for troubled youths in the vein of St. Mary's, arguing that keeping families together for the "sake of the family" is not always in the best interest of the child.

Mara expressed his frustration by highlighting the plight of some teens on the hockey team he coached. Of the five starters on his 2006 team, all of them had adult criminal records. "Three of the five boys have never had lasting interactions with their fathers, and four of them have mothers suffering long term heroin addiction," he said. "Two of the young men have two addicted parents while only one of the parents I have known has had a job. And they all come from a single block of North Glover Street in east Baltimore.

"And so, the question I have for the reader is this," he concludes. "What was the purpose of keeping families such as these intact?"[4]

What must be done for these children? Is it ultimately better to remove a child from their home or imprison them—for his or her own good, and the good of society?

And what about the parents? At the correctional facility I work at, I am frequently dismayed to learn that an inmate's father is in an adjoining unit at the same jail. What can be done to stop the cycle of criminal behavior and violence from continuing on down through each new generation?

Mara's frustration is echoed by thousands of police, prosecutors, social service and child welfare workers. When a child does bad things—and they do—what do we as responsible adults and caretakers do with them? Do we scold them, wagging a finger and telling them not to repeat the behavior? Or is there some form of punishment that can satisfy the victim while rehabilitating the perpetrator?

This question has been hotly debated for the past generation. Over the centuries, society has made various attempts at juvenile justice and rehabilitation, but little has been done in the realm of early identification and treatment. What's more, some "rehabilitation centers" become something more akin to warehouses, places where there is little rehabilitation and even further exposure to crime and victimization. The Florida School for Boys was notorious for allegations and proven instances of sexual abuse, beatings, torture, and neglect, all of which do little to reform children and only serve to help them graduate to a life of adult criminal behavior. The mere term "reform school," which should give the impression that serious attempts are made at rehabilitating juvenile offenders, now only serves as a euphemism for jailing children.

One popular juvenile offender reformer was Father Edward Flanagan, a Roman Catholic priest based in Omaha, Nebraska. Seeing a need to reform wayward children from a position of empathy, caring, and social preparation through education, job/skill training, and self-reliance, he founded Boys Town in 1917. The thirty-one-year-old bespectacled Irish immigrant was a noted pragmatist, and his observations still hold true today: "There are no bad boys (or girls). There is only bad environment, bad training, bad example, bad thinking."

These risk factors *can* propel a child into delinquency and acts of violence, certainly. But what about the child who commits a violent act while coming from a seemingly loving and nurturing home with two involved parents?

Such was the case of Erin Caffey. The Caffeys, who lived in Emory, Texas, appeared to be a close-knit Christian family dedicated to their church. Erin even sang in the church's choir. In the early hours of March 1, 2008, their seemingly ideal life tragically collapsed. A pair of gunmen entered the house, killing Caffey's mother, Penny, 37; and her brothers, Matthew, 13, and Tyler, 8. Her father Terry was shot multiple times but survived his injuries. As if this wasn't heinous enough, the assailants then set fire to the house, hoping to cover their crime.

It was only when the smoke cleared that sixteen-year-old Erin was revealed to have been the one who lit the proverbial fuse setting in motion the murder of her family. The leader of the gunmen was revealed to be her eighteen-year-old boyfriend who, along with his twenty-year-old friend, had entered the house and systematically begun shooting Erin's family on her orders, while she and another male teen sat in a vehicle outside. Erin was motivated by her parents' disapproval of her relationship with the older boy.

Erin later told television host Piers Morgan, "When I look back on it now, this was all just stupid. I mean, for what? They weren't beating me, they weren't starving me to death. I had it made."[5]

If Erin's statement makes your brow furrow in bewilderment, it shouldn't. Acts of teen violence often have inexplicable motives which, in the not as-yet fully developed brain of an adolescent, makes perfect sense. They don't comprehend their motives and can't conceive of the consequences of their actions.

Don't get me wrong—I'm not making apologies for these perpetrators. Nor am I ignorant to the fact that young people are capable of pure evil. Teens commit violent acts for a myriad of reasons, whether out of anger, impaired judgement through alcohol/and or drugs, jealousy, fear of having a bad act revealed to a parent or authority figure, selfishness, gang representation/retribution, in the commission of another crime such as a home break-in or drug deal gone bad...the list goes on.

There are many cases where a juvenile demonstrates absolutely no forethought (or indeed afterthought) for their actions. They show little to no remorse, a complete lack of appreciation for the impact of their actions. Some of this can be attributed to environment while some of it can be attributed to the impairment of brain development as a result to being exposed to alcohol and/or drugs while in the womb.

There are also a host of causes for juvenile violence that have little to nothing to do with the individual themselves. Mental illness and brain trauma have a direct influence on child behavior, as does fetal alcohol or fetal drug withdrawal syndromes.

Another area that needs to be considered is the environment that govern children with special needs, especially emotional disorders—a critical area that needs extensive attention in terms of identification and appropriate treatment, not only in the school but at home. A disturbingly large number of children are exposed to unspeakable dysfunctions at home, such as violence, sexual abuse and even exploitation. It's hard to comprehend, but it does occur: a parent can sell their child's innocence to strangers in return for drugs, rendering them victims of post-traumatic stress disorder.

In other cases, parents or family members are incarcerated, leaving a void in the domestic nurturing cycle which can spark behavioral reactions. Exposure to domestic violence has been reported to create a multi-generational cycle of violence among children. Drug and alcohol abuse leading to child neglect is among the most heartbreaking circumstances a child can be forced to endure. Again, the list goes on. Life is an endless uphill battle for tens of thousands of children. And we wonder why some choose to lash out in violent acts. Some, but not all; determining the difference between the two groups may well be the key to understanding and hopefully counteracting the threat of teen violence. However, we will see that violent responses are typically motivated not just by one contributing factor, but by the accumulation of multiple factors which ultimately causes the pressure cooker to blow.

The purpose of the book is two-fold. First, to identify those circumstances that can place a child at risk for violent behavior, and learn what ignites this predilection towards violent action; and second, to explore strategies that can be employed to mitigate the damage and put them on a positive life track. This is not an easy task. While there is a plethora of gurus who claim to have the magical elixir to "fix" a violent child, the fact is there is not one single element that can work. Strategies must take a holistic approach, one which involves parents, domestic, educational, and social environments, proper access to resources, and support mechanisms to help keep the juvenile on track to being law-abiding and productive.

This includes, but is not limited to, completing an educational track that will make these children employable. While many parents and school officials attempt to push students towards college, this may only serve to set the student up for more pressure and unrealistic expectations. The reality is that college is not a panacea for all social ills, nor is it a guarantee of future prospects. Then there are the troubled students who get labeled and are forgotten altogether, left to fall through the cracks. There are many high-paying trades that at-risk students deserve the option and tools to explore. In fact, many union-type trade skills pay better than what a typical college graduate will ever make. Employment guidance and resources are still key to demonstrating to the individual that there is hope for the future—hope for a "normal" life, and that they can break out of whatever dysfunctional domestic circumstances have contributed to their at-risk state.

This book is not a step-by-step cookbook. There are always unknown variables that can contribute to violent behavior which require the reader to avoid pigeonholing a child under a suspected causative factor. This establishes the need for attempting those strategies which are most appropriate, which in turn makes the inclusion of the juvenile in the reform process absolutely crucial. They need to be given the opportunity to not only buy in but *control* their own destiny. It must be remembered that many of these teens are street smart beyond the capabilities of those new to working with at-risk youth. They are shrewd and can be manipulative. They are also part of sub-cultures—such as gangs—which are steeped in respect. Despite the thousands of well-trained and intentioned teachers adept at managing disruptive students, we often see a failure by many educators to grasp these facts due to a lack of foreknowledge and appreciation.

What this book will also not be, at least in the eyes of many, is "politically correct". It is this social phenomenon which I feel has obfuscated any constructive dialogue as to the causative factors and demographics of violent juvenile crime. You can't fix a problem if you refuse to identify it or make excuses for those committing the crimes.

Since the late 1960s there has been a linear regression of respect for authority and law in the United States, with a concurrent lack of accountability. We see this in current political discourse, where conversation has been replaced with social media bullying by the very people who are supposed to be leaders and pillars of our society and government. What lesson does this send to vulnerable youth? When parents fail to guide their children along the right path of personal and social responsibility, and the children are reprimanded by someone in authority—say, a teacher or police officer—the parents are up in arms, making excuses for their children and denying outright they could have done anything wrong. In this situation, the only lesson learned is one of a lack of personal responsibility and accountability.

We must take a full and unapologetic look at every factor which contributes to the sort of moral bankruptcy needed before a teenager decides to pick up a gun and shoot another person in the face before nonchalantly walking away. If we are seriously intent on protecting our children, we need to look at the entire child and what their real needs are.

It is my hope this book's overview of the complexity of youth violence will add to the conversation and help develop new strategies for mitigating teen violence. But before we can begin trying to solve the problem, we must cultivate a better understanding of just how bad things have gotten over the last fifty years.

CHAPTER 1

THE GREATEST HORROR: UNDERSTANDING THE FACTS OF JUVENILE VIOLENCE

"America is now home to thickening ranks of juvenile 'super predators'—radically impulsive, brutally remorseless youngsters, including ever more pre-teenage boys who murder, assault, rob, burglarize, deal deadly drugs, join gun-toting gangs, and create serious communal disorder."
—WILLIAM J. BENNETT, JOHN J. DIIULIO,
AND JOHN P. WALTERS[1]

THERE IS NOTHING glamorous about statistics, especially when it comes to crime—in particular, violent juvenile crime. This element of our society is often obscured by school and civic officials who would prefer to avoid any stain on their institution, one which may reflect policy failures they'd rather were left unidentified, as this can have potential adverse effects on enrollment, funding, housing, and economic development.

Then there are the parents who will ignorantly (or deliberately) ignore the failings of their children rather than attempt to rectify and guide them onto the right path. Absent from most figures as well is the consequence of the violent action on a victim, their family, and the surrounding community, as well as the impact on the juvenile offender's current and future plight, their family, and the criminal justice system.

Nevertheless, data is necessary to paint a picture of what has occurred, where it occurred, how it occurred, how we can use that information to predict future criminal behavior, and how we can employ solutions to address the crimes.

Unfortunately, data is also used (and abused) for political means, neglecting both victim and perpetrator. When I was in college, I had to take a statistics class. Ironically, the title of the textbook was *How to Lie with Statistics*[2] by Darrell Huff. Being a naïve freshman, I had assumed that data was the epitome of facts; that intellectual conversation and policy could only be based upon cold, hard statistical information. That presumption was quickly dashed when I read the textbook's introduction: "The secret language of statistics, so appealing in a fact-minded culture, is employed to sensationalize, inflate, confuse, and oversimplify," wrote Huff[3], who contends that statistics are openly vulnerable to agendas, manipulation, and bias.

As we see in many contemporary social issues ranging from gun control, to abortion, to immigration, pundits are notorious for manipulating data to fit their agenda. So it is with violent juvenile crime as well. A wealth of data exists that shows a surprising decrease in violent crime as a whole over time[4]. But what the data fails to account for is the rise in *specific* violent crimes such as school shootings and gang crime, both of which are focal points in current political rhetoric.

According to the Office of Justice Programs' Office of Juvenile Justice and Delinquency Prevention (OJJDP), a subsection of the Department of Justice: between 1980 and 2015, there has been a steady decline of juvenile offender homicide cases, with the peak year being 1994 (with 2,340 reported cases). The data is further broken down to 1,335 homicides committed by an individual juvenile; 273 with multiple juvenile suspects; and 712 homicides committed with an adult[5]. This data also coincides with the height of the crack cocaine phenomenon.

By 2013, the juvenile homicide rate hit a twenty-three year low with a cumulative 613 cases. However, by 2015 the juvenile homicide rate has begun creeping up again, with 356 homicides being committed solely by a juvenile; 66 committed with multiple juveniles; and 264 homicides committed with adults, for a total of 686.

Demographically, the homicide rate was dominated by sixteen and seventeen-year-old African-American juveniles[6]. The latter demographic involved mostly black-on-black crime, which underscores another social dilemma many in the political arena have completely failed to address, especially during the Black Lives Matter movement post-Ferguson.

The perception that there is an epidemic of African-American homicides at the hands of racially insensitive police was found to be completely erroneous, yet activists and politicians persisted in perpetuating the myth, which only served to obscure the reality of a mounting body count of young African-American males in Chicago and a generation of black-on-black violent crime in Washington, D.C. In her book *War on Cops*, Heather MacDonald attempted to bring parity to the conversation regarding the realities of homicides against African-Americans[7]. MacDonald found, amid the outcry against police, that fourteen to seventeen-year-old African-American males were murdered at six times the rate of whites and Hispanics combined, and *not* by police. In Chicago, the situation is even worse for children, despite an improved homicide rate for adults—one in every five people murdered in Chicago is eighteen years old or younger[8].

While these numbers are an incredibly disturbing commentary on a specific population of American citizens, the outrage expressed by activists and politicians over this information is deafening in its silence—for to do any different would mean admitting the failure of their own agendas and policies.

An indisputable study by the Centers for Disease Control and Prevention found that between 2002–2014, African-American children were ten times more likely to die from guns than white children[9].

Offense Charged	Number of persons arrested					
	Under 18 years of age			18 years of age and over		
	2005	2014	Percent change	2005	2014	Percent change
Murder and nonnegligent manslaughter	598	331	-44.6	5,889	4,598	-21.9
Rape	1,786	1,501	-	10,101	8,256	-
Robbery	13,790	9,150	-33.6	40,732	37,606	-7.7
Aggravated assault	29,145	14,908	-48.8	194,395	172,316	-11.4
Burglary	39,843	20,602	-48.3	111,952	106,301	-5.0
Larceny-theft	144,688	83,438	-42.3	412,118	503,783	+22.2
Motor vehicle theft	16,121	5,142	-68.1	51,027	28,111	-44.9
Arson	4,065	1,547	-61.9	4,020	3,137	-22.0
Violent crime	45,319	25,890	-42.9	251,117	222,776	-11.3
Property crime	204,717	110,729	-45.9	579,117	641,332	+10.7
Other assaults	114,737	63,260	-44.9	458,822	425,745	-7.2

Yet the FBI's Uniformed Crime Report, which is released annually, demonstrated markedly different trends. It is worth mentioning that the data portrayed in these reports is based on what is submitted by law enforcement agencies, and it is reasonable to presume that there are homicide cases that go unreported.

In 2014, there were 331 juvenile non-negligent homicides[10]. This report shines a light of optimism by revealing nearly a forty-five percent drop in juvenile homicides from a decade earlier. No explanations are given as to why this may be, but the ray of hope was short-lived; by 2016, the rate of juvenile homicides more than doubled, to 682[11].

Further data from the Centers for Disease Control and Prevention are just as bleak. Homicide rates increased twenty-seven percent between 2014 and 2016, after declining thirty-five percent between 2007 and 2014[12].

Not surprisingly, researchers found the leading cause of homicide in 2016 were firearms. This fuels the rhetoric over gun control but doesn't take into account how children get their hands on weapons despite legislators attempting to make it more difficult for adults to obtain a gun.

The OJJDP's numbers provide a clear message regarding how juvenile murder rates crept up in the eighties and peaked in the nineties. The causes for this increase will be discussed in later chapters; suffice it to say, violent crime can be directly related to the proliferation of drugs on the streets of America in the late 60s and 70s, creating a lucrative yet life-threatening cash cow to poor urban teens.

To provide a bit more context: in 1960, before the social upheaval and transformation of traditional norms in the U.S. were challenged by progressive movements in that era, the juvenile homicide rate was less than 4 per 100,000 people[13]. In 1977, the homicide rate for juveniles had slightly increased to 7.2 per 100,000 people. But by 1994, in the same span of time as between the first two figures, the rate has leapt up to 19.1[14]. What happened to juveniles during this period? There was always juvenile delinquency and even violent crime, but nothing on the scale of what would emerge during the so-called "Age of Aquarius" during the 60s and 70s.

In 1993, James Alan Fox, Ph.D., Dean of Criminal Justice at Northeastern University in Boston wrote, "The causes for the surge in youth violence since the mid-1980s reach, of course, well beyond demographics. There have been tremendous changes in the social context of crime over the past decade, which explains why this generation of youth is more violent than others before it. This generation of youth has more dangerous drugs in their bodies, more deadly weapons in their hands, and a seemingly more casual attitude about violence"[15].

This level of crime is reflective not only of a disregard for humanity but also for authority. Take, for example, the case of Dwanta Anthony Harris, a sixteen-year-old charged with the first-degree murder of a female Baltimore police officer.

Described by the presiding judge as a "one-man crime wave"[16], Harris was accused of murdering Officer Amy Caprio during her response to a suspicious vehicle call in the northeast Baltimore community of Perry Hall in May 2018. When Caprio arrived around 2 PM, she followed Harris, who was in the driver seat of a stolen black Jeep Wrangler, to a cul-de-sac outside a house that his three associates were inside, burglarizing. Caprio drew her weapon and told Harris to get out of the vehicle. Rather than obey the officer, the belligerent sixteen-year-old feigned compliance and opened the door, but then immediately shut it again, ducked down in the front driver seat, and bore down on the accelerator, intentionally striking Caprio, who did get a shot off, which struck the Jeep's windshield. Harris fled the scene but was later captured, alongside his accomplices fifteen-year-old Darrell Jaymar Ward; sixteen-year-old Derrick Eugene Matthews; and Eugene Robert Genius IV, all of whom were not only charged as adults in the commission of a burglary, but with the first-degree murder of Caprio[17].

On the surface, Harris' case appears to be yet another failure of the juvenile justice system. His criminal history, which likely prompted the judge's comment about him being a "one-man crime wave," showed he had been implicated in four previous auto thefts and was actually placed on house arrest with an electronic ankle monitor the month before he killed Caprio. But less than two weeks before he killed Caprio, there was a detention hearing held for Harris where, without the department's knowledge, he was released with electronic monitoring[18] only to run away four days later. As a matter of fact, he was wearing the ankle monitor at the time he ran over Caprio[19]. Officials said they attempted to locate Harris after he left his home via his monitor, but the device only identified whether he was in or outside his house, not his geographic location.

On top of the increased incidence of juvenile offenders, there is also the increase in the number of juvenile victims to consider. The OJJDP released a report in 2001[20] that describes the figures relating to juvenile victims. According to the authors: "Homicide is the only major cause of childhood death that has increased in incidence during the past thirty years. While deaths of children resulting from accidents, congenital defects, and infectious diseases were falling, homicides of children were increasing"[21]. It is worth mentioning that an undisclosed number of these victims could have been murdered by a suspect who would not be considered a juvenile. Nevertheless, the end result was a dead child. We must also account for those children who were physically and/or emotionally wounded by violence, and the impact this has on their future.

As mentioned earlier, data can paint whatever picture the user wishes. For this reason, it is the lifeblood of academics searching for answers to formulate prevention strategies and policy makers looking to reactively address trends through resource allocation. We are currently seeing this in the wake of multiple school shooter tragedies, as politicians scramble to eradicate guns, beef up school security, investigate student mental health, etc.

Unfortunately, our society has a tendency to be reactive rather than proactive. Many of the violent crimes committed by adolescents *are* preventable. There is no evidence of a tectonic shift in human evolution that causes our brains to act differently. What has changed, and changed dramatically, are our social norms and mores.

Data can also serve to keep unpleasant things we'd rather not consider in the realm of the abstract. Even when there are drops in the rate of violent juvenile crime, how *much* of a drop should we consider "satisfactory" if children are still killing and being killed? What is an "acceptable" number of juvenile homicides?

Of course, the ideal number is zero, but that is unrealistic. These numbers become much more compelling when there are names and faces attached, when the impact these tragedies have on the families involved is brought to the forefront.

How do you reconcile the "data" of twenty children killed at Sandy Hook Elementary School in 2012, or fourteen at Stoneman Douglas High School in 2018? You can't; yet these young faces and names of destroyed lives become reduced to cold figures in a criminologist's graph of juvenile violence or a talking point for a politician advocating for gun control or strategies to prevent the next tragedy.

Data cannot be allowed to distract from the human element of the crime—the human cost, and the human consequence. Where data *can* be useful is to help identify the most at-risk populations for either being victimized by juvenile violence or perpetrating it. The reasons for this will be discussed in later chapters, but according to the data, different types of violence are unique to different demographics. For example: why are the majority of street homicides committed by African-American juveniles? Why are the majority of mass school shootings done by white suburban teens? The associated causative factors can be based on socio-economic status, homelife, mental disability, substance abuse, prescription medication side effects, etc.

For instance, consider eighteen-year-old Eric Harris and seventeen-year-old Dylan Klebold, who in 1999 systematically walked through Columbine High School in Colorado killing twelve students and a teacher. Not only did this represent the start of a new millennium but also the dawn of copycat school tragedies, all using guns, with the majority of suspects being white. Bullying served as the underpinning for many of these incidents; but why is mass murder now, in this generation, an option for dealing with one's hurt feelings?

Kids have always been bullied; were previous generations simply better at adversarial coping than the current generation? The answers are elusive and, more importantly, go much deeper than the numbers can say.

Violence does need to be personalized to better express the impact it has on individuals and society. Data should form a framework to demonstrate how pervasive a problem is and indicate a strategic direction. Consider this: statistically speaking, active school shooting deaths are statistically lower compared to the number of reported murders in the U.S. They are also only calculated as individual homicides on the Uniform Crime Reports, not as the massacres they are, which results in the numbers being numerically overshadowed by other incidents. Compare the impact of eight murdered students in a high school shooting to three children, ages two, eleven and twelve, killed in Chicago in the span of four days in February 2017[22].

Through the haze of numbers and data, consider the victims who are virtually unknown or forgotten to all but their families, who are perhaps never named in the media. Consider two-year-old Lovontay White and his family, or eleven-year-old Takiya Holmes; or the victims and families of Columbine High School, Sandy Hook Elementary School, and every other school related shooting. Their ignominious association with these tragedies in the form of nothing but crime data provides no benefit unless that data is put to constructive and operational use to prevent other children from joining the ranks of crime victim statistics.

CONCLUSION

The increased incidence of teen crime is a reflection of many failed social norms and policies, all of which is borne out in vivid detail by data collected by state and federal law agencies. But while this

data can be beneficial in strategically implementing prevention and suppression strategies, this is only the case when used sincerely, and not as a tool to push a political agenda—which does little to directly rectify the propensity we're seeing for youth criminal activity. This data should provide the impetus for short and long-term strategies that can in turn be supported by data. By the same token, the subjective impact of data-driven crime prevention strategies can't be ignored, either.

CHAPTER 2

UNRAVELING THE MYSTERY: RISK FACTORS AND CAUSES OF JUVENILE VIOLENCE

"A person is born with feelings of envy and hate. If he gives way to them, they will lead him to violence and crime, and any sense of loyalty and good faith will be abandoned."
—Xunzi, Confucian philosopher

EXAMPLES OF VIOLENT behavior among young people dates all the way back to Biblical times, to the second generation of humans. In the story of Cain and Abel, we see the two brothers fall victim to one of man's most basic failings—jealousy. The Book of Genesis says that God preferred the sacrifices offered by Abel, a shepherd, over those of his older brother Cain, a farmer. Incensed, Cain sought retribution and murdered his sibling, and was sentenced to wander the earth forevermore.

A sentence which, unfortunately, is all-too-common among many of today's violent youths, who aimlessly wander the earth both in body and spirit, through little fault of their own and due to circumstances they had no control over. Recall Father Flanagan's words: "There are no bad boys (or girls). There is only bad environment, bad training, bad example, bad thinking." Our current culture doesn't want to acknowledge this. There is always an institution to blame, such as the schools, or child protective services, or the media, or music, video games, movies, etc. Yet despite bearing the brunt of blame, these institutions didn't invent the aberrant behavior that turns children into killers.

Most children will act out and challenge adult authority as they enter adolescence. This is a natural part of growing up, an unavoidable aspect of human nature. Their exposure to certain risk factors throughout their childhood has a direct impact on their behavior, as well as the presence or absence of guidance in determining right and wrong behavior, behavioral boundaries, societal expectations, and a proper understanding of the consequences of their behavior. All of these variables must be factored in when determining how a juvenile will react to an incident that could trigger violent behavior.

In this chapter, we open the door to the myriad risk factors children face that can incite violent behavior, as well as the warning signs to watch for and what can be done as emergency stop-gaps before an act of violence tragically unfolds. Violent actions by juveniles are commonly a result of the *accumulation* of many of these risk factors, triggered by a seemingly benign incident. A juvenile who shoots up a school because he was bullied may have shown underlying depression or poor coping mechanisms before a random episode pushed them over the edge. A juvenile who kills another teen in a bad drug deal was likely brought there because of the poverty that forced him to sell drugs to survive, or parental neglect, or the perception that they were disrespected. Through a better understanding of the foundation of juvenile violence, we are better prepared to spot the warning signs and work to counteract the potential risk factors.

ENVIRONMENT

A child's "environment" encompasses many realms. It includes aspects of their physical environment, such as quality of housing, economic status of the family and how that may impact proper developmental nutrition, or risk of exposure to harmful chemicals. For example, it has been postulated that exposure to lead during pregnancy and lead poisoning, especially among African-American and (to some extent) Hispanic families in low-income housing projects, is connected to an increased number of arrests for violent offenses. In a study of 250 subjects that looked at individuals from birth to ages 19–24 years old, researchers found that the more lead in a child's blood at six years old, the higher their chances of being arrested for a violent crime as a young adult[1]. These findings were corroborated in other studies as well[2,3].

Interestingly, a report that put a specific timeline to the effect of lead exposure on crime found that, as the exposure to lead—both in the form of lead-based paint and vehicle fumes—decreased in the 1970s and 80s, the crime rate decreased as well, become noticeably lower by the 1990s[4]. As we recall from the previous chapter, violent crime among juveniles started dramatically increasing between 1988–1994 and didn't decline to pre-1984 levels until 2004[5]. Herbert L. Needleman and his colleagues studied 194 delinquent children in Allegheny County, PA, who were arrested and adjudicated by the Juvenile Court, alongside 146 non-delinquent children. The researchers found that the "delinquent" children were four times more likely to have suffered lead poisoning than the non-delinquent youth. This result held true even after looking at other problems that affect delinquency, including the level of parental education and employment, single-parent households, number of children living in the home, and neighborhood crime rates.[6]

One exposure that has received inadequate examination is the retrospective analysis of juvenile criminal behavior of children exposed to drugs, such as crack and methamphetamine while in utero. In 2013, Wendell reported 750,000 cases of pregnant women who had taken drugs while pregnant[7]. This fetal exposure can have a direct relationship to behavioral problems such as difficulties with self-regulation and deficits in some aspects of cognitive performance, information processing, and sustained attention to tasks[8].

According to Dr. Linda LaGasse at the Warren Alpert Medical School of Brown University and Women and Infants Hospital in Providence, Rhode Island, methamphetamine use during pregnancy can disrupt the normal development of the frontal cortex. Disrupted frontal cortex circuitry may impair inhibitory control, which in turn may lead to attention deficits and behavioral problems[9].

Environmental variables such as family dysfunction, parents and family members being involved in criminal or risky behaviors, domestic violence, divorce, lack of developmental guidance, and more can all serve to contribute to a child's violent behavior. In the following pages, we'll address each potential risk factor, how to identify them and what can be done to address or mitigate their influence.

THEORETICAL FOUNDATION FOR CRIMINAL BEHAVIOR

Before beginning a thorough examination of the possible risk factors and causes of juvenile violence, it may be helpful to review theories regarding the origins of criminal behavior.

Over the decades, sociologists have attempted to identify causative explanations for criminal behavior. How much of a factor is one's home environment? One's social environment? Economic status? Ethnic/racial composition?

These theories do not seek to conclusively explain human criminal behavior; rather, they look to provide likely explanations for the cumulative effect of social exposures.

Social Strain Theory refers to the means by which an individual decides to achieve an objective, and whether these means are legally and socially acceptable[10]. For example, a teenager sees a nice car he wants. Rather than work hard to earn the money to buy it, he decides to steal it. Or, something which has been occurring since the emergence of designer sneakers in the mid to late eighties: rather than save money, teens have accosted others (in many cases violently), and stolen the shoes right off their victim's feet.

Differential Association Theory is the idea that criminal behavior is learned. Through interaction with others, individuals learn certain values, attitudes, and techniques that can lead to or encourage criminal behavior. Frequently seen in children exposed to criminal behavior in their home or social circle, they come to believe that the behavior is actually acceptable[11], resulting in an aberrated sense of normalcy. I once saw this in a seventeen-year-old member of a violent street gang in Albuquerque, who was placed in a gang diversion program as an alternative to jail. "I really want to get out of the gang but it's hard because my dad and uncles are all gang members," he told me. "I learned a lot here, but I still have to go home after this."

Social Disorganization Theory explains criminal behavior as a direct result of one's immediate surroundings; the environment in which you live determines the likelihood of your participating in criminal activity. This is perhaps the most relevant attempt to justify criminal behavior as it relates to poverty[12]. The theory goes that while an individual can distinguish between legal and illegal activity, the poverty around overwhelms them, causing an erosion of social organization. Poverty is also related to unemployment and underemployment, which puts strain on the family structure and can lead to domestic dysfunction, single parent households, and poor supervision of children[13]. Look at any impoverished community and see how this impacts life. Vandalism, public intoxication, drug abuse and crime are endemic in a life where there is little hope or opportunity. Of course, there *are* families who valiantly struggle to maintain control of their children through a value system at home, but this is often thwarted as soon as they hit the streets and associate with friends who see anti-social behavior as a means to survive. Peer pressure is a strong impulse for teens to overcome.

Routine Activity Theory is pertinent to our current discussion. It argues that an individual's social surroundings, and whether that environment mitigates or exacerbates criminal behavior[14], is the determining factor in whether an individual engages in criminal acts. Hillary Rodham Clinton makes a reasonable suggestion in *It Takes a Village*[15] but the reality is most "villages" don't have the planning or resources in place to address the needs of all kids, especially high-risk individuals. Modern society has made this ideal into a daunting task. In lower income households, parents (whether single parent or both parents) will both be working one, maybe two or more jobs. This reduces the likelihood of proper child supervision, and the more at-risk they are, the greater risk of criminal behavior.

There are gaps in these theoretical explanations, particularly in explaining certain violent behaviors in teens. Not all teen killers are from poor backgrounds, or single-family homes, or have been directly exposed to criminal influences. Theories are based on research and observations of available academic information. Once again, the specter of data interpretation sneaks back into the discussion.

Poverty and/or family dysfunction should not be an excuse for criminal behavior. I have known many people, some within my own family, who have risen above poverty and adverse home lives to get undergraduate and graduate degrees and become responsible and contributing members of society. My grandfather, an Italian immigrant, always told us that the kids on his block in Little Italy, New York either became policemen, priests, or criminals. (This was in the era of the notorious Black Hand, which has strikingly similar characteristics to MS13 a century later.)

My grandfather became a New York City Police detective. Following his retirement, he became a successful businessman. He always instilled in us that the poverty and ethnic adversity he overcame motivated him to work harder, and never served as an excuse to become a criminal. This principle still exists in contemporary society, but unfortunately receives little more than lip service. While attempting to continue this principle, we undercut ourselves by making excuses for bad behavior—whether on the level of a minor school infraction, all the way to serious crimes like murder. Criminal charges are frequently reduced (through the use of plea bargains at the judicial stage) for the sake of expediency. I've seen inmates at the correctional facility I work at laugh at their sentences, often seeing it as a badge of honor. When they break the rules and face additional sanctions, they nonchalantly reply that they are already facing thirty, forty years in jail, so who cares? This is a challenging mindset to try and thwart.

It is for these reasons that I want to discuss other causes of violent juvenile behavior—causes that all parents, educators, and social welfare officials should be sensitive towards *before* a homicide occurs.

BOREDOM

In 2017, twenty-two-year-old Marquise Byrd of Warren, Michigan was enjoying Christmas. It was a great time; he was preparing to get engaged to the mother of his two-year-old son and his brother had just returned from a military deployment.

He never made it to 2018. While a passenger in a vehicle driving on Interstate 75 in downtown Toledo, Ohio, a sandbag came crashing through the window, striking him in the head. Byrd would later die in a local hospital. Four teenagers, three of them fourteen years of age and the other thirteen, would later be arrested and charged with his murder[16]. The teens had been throwing sandbags and debris onto the busy interstate as a way to amuse themselves.

In my hometown of Albuquerque, New Mexico, a beautiful city renowned for its balloon fiesta, the Sandia Mountain range, and a lush desert landscape, we are also plagued with multiple acts of senseless violence that fit into this category of juvenile boredom-turned-homicidal. There is a large homeless/transient population here, many of whom are Native Americans coming to the city to escape the stringent alcohol prohibition laws on the reservations.

On two separate occasions in recent memory, juveniles fatally attacked these vulnerable victims. The first attack came in July 2014, when three bored teens—Alez Rios, 18, Nathaniel Carrillo, 16, and Gilbert Tafoya, 15—went to an abandoned lot on Central Avenue and 60th Street on the city's west side and approached three homeless Navajo men in their makeshift camp, where they systematically began striking the helpless men in the head with cinder blocks, bricks and whatever else they could get their hands on. Two men died; the other, Jerome Eskeets, got away. He later said that the teens approached them with their faces covered. "They were giggling and laughing at us, mocking us, calling us homeless. I said, 'I don't know why you guys are bothering us. We didn't do nothing to you guys.'"[17].

Even hardened investigators were taken aback by the depravity shown in the murders. "They are unrecognizable," Simon Drobik, an Albuquerque Police Department spokesman, said of the victims. "My question is: Who failed these kids? How did it get to this point? It was so violent. I was sick to my stomach. Homicide [detectives] had a hard time dealing with it"[18].

The motive for this horrendous attack makes even less sense. According to police, Tafoya was upset that he and his girlfriend had broken up and he felt the need to beat someone up. It later emerged that this lame excuse bore little relevance to how depraved these three teens were. Tafoya admitted to police the trio had attacked some fifty homeless people in recent months[19].

The second attack occurred in March 2018, when two teens shot a homeless man multiple times—again, for fun. Timothy Chavez, 15, and Anthony Gallegos, 17, were at a birthday party at the Crowne Plaza Hotel at Menaul Boulevard and University NE in Albuquerque, where they were reportedly flashing a handgun. Bored, Chavez left the party and walked along Menaul Avenue, a busy street, when he came across fifty-year-old Ronnie Ross. By all accounts, there had been no previous contact between the teens and Ross. Regardless, Chavez shot Ross then nonchalantly went back to the party to tell Gallegos he shot a "hobo". Not believing his friend, the pair went back to Ross, who was bleeding and dying on the street as vehicles drove by, and once again shot him multiple times. When it was over, the victim had been shot a dozen times—a random victim who police said was murdered "for fun"[20]. "They killed an individual for fun," police said. "Both of them shot this individual six times"[21].

This is just a sampling of bored teens run amok resorting to grotesque violence to fill a void in their lives the adults around them failed to teach or demonstrate how to constructively fill. Teen "boredom" is not unusual; it is almost a rite of passage between childhood and adulthood, a time to reprogram the mind for more mature endeavors. No matter where a teen lives, whether in a bustling city with multiple opportunities or on a rural farm, they will all, at some point complain of boredom. It's what is done with that emotion that will make a difference for the rest of their, and potentially someone else's, life.

In some cases, communities, schools, and organizations such as sports clubs, after school programs, or the Boys and Girls Club can attempt to fill these voids with programs to nurture creativity and physical fitness. In lieu of organized activities, parents need to spend quality time with their children—not just to be together but to spend the time it takes to teach valuable life lessons. The problem isn't the availability of programs, it is access to them. Parents have to sign kids up and take them to where the program group meets, which can be challenging when they work or just don't care. Inaccessibility to creative resources can and often will lead to delinquency, but it most definitely should not be deadly.

In other cases, if the teen does not know how to fill the void in their life, they will turn to the ubiquitous electronic devices. While this may satisfy their boredom for a brief time and take pressure off parents to entertain their children, this practice is not without its consequences. In moderation, electronic devices can be enjoyable, but when they become an obsession at the expense of personal health and hygiene or creating an alternative environment, they become detrimental. Carl E. Pickhardt, Ph.D., writing about boredom in Psychology Today in 2012[22], said that while boredom among teens is normal, it should not be ignored, either: "Tolerance for boredom, particularly among adolescents, has been greatly reduced in a world where escape into the many screens of electronic entertainment is so easily accomplished. We have created a culture in which many young children and adolescents have grown used to being electronically over-stimulated from birth, a condition that makes meeting the offline routine and repetitive demands of home and school difficult for many of them to endure. And as on-line escape increasingly substitutes for off-line engagement, as virtual world competence is gained at the expense of real-world experience, practice dealing with real life challenges, shouldering real life responsibilities, and developing real life skills can decline. Paying attention and sitting still for offline demands can feel really boring to do"[23].

Children/adolescents are increasingly unable to cope with "real world" crises and may respond in unacceptable and even violent ways especially if they are with a criminal cohort of acquaintances. This is what had played out with the Albuquerque teens where unprovoked acts of violence were necessary to fill their voids.

ABNORMAL BRAIN FUNCTION

Whether it is a group of teens throwing sandbags off a freeway overpass or beating homeless people to death, there is clearly a physiological developmental component contributing to the ambivalence towards actions and consequences observable in modern teenagers. Our brain isn't fully developed until we reach about twenty-three years old and is extremely fragile to external influences, whether from environment or physical injury. Researchers agree that the body of a child who is exposed to stress and violence will release a flood of hormones in order to protect itself from the stressor, be it exposure to domestic dysfunction or violence. Many children who commit homicides fit into this categories, which offers some explanation for their behavior.

One major area where behavior can become compromised is impulse control. Children exposed to these situations may be quick to react in a hyper state of vigilance, lashing out without full appreciation for the consequences or empathy for their victim. There may also be issues of dissociation, where they reflexively act in an aggressive manner that they think is appropriate[24]. This hyper vigilant state will present itself in situations where a teen is sitting around bored while recent stressors, like Tafoya breaking up with his girlfriend, percolate and build until being released in whatever manner they see fit—usually violently.

The consequences of traumatic brain injury must also be included in the conversation. Instances of single or repeated trauma to the brain can have a profound impact on behavior, as seen in cases where a seemingly "good" teen sustains a TBI in a car or athletic accident, and begins manifesting anti-social behavior. Among the symptoms of repeated exposure to TBI is the inability to control anger[25]; according to prison data, inmates have as much as ten times the exposure to TBIs as the non-prison population[26].

In an article for *Brain Injury Professional Magazine,* author Jean Langlois expands on this point, saying, "The problem of TBI and violence is complicated by the fact that violence is not only a cause, but a consequence of TBI. Specifically, TBI-related cognitive and behavioral problems can also result in aggressive behavior that leads to perpetration of violence, or a lack of insight and judgment, and resulting vulnerability, that can lead to victimization"[27].

Experts advocate testing of inmates for TBI, but this is rarely done. Which is unfortunate, as doing so would allow for an appropriate treatment program to be implemented both during and after incarceration. Neglecting to do this ignores one of the root causes of what got the individual in trouble in the first place and can contribute to recidivism (the repeated commission of criminal acts, contributing to the revolving door of a lifetime of incarceration).

For as much as trauma and even tumors on or in the brain can affect behavior, officials are now also re-examining how even a healthy juvenile brain can be impacted when a crime is committed because, as stated, the brain still has yet to fully develop. The "healthy but immature brain" defense is gaining momentum, with the most notorious suspect in recent history being Dzokhar Tsarnaev, charged with the 2013 Boston Marathon bombing. Although he was nineteen at the time of the horrendous attack that left four dead and some

264 wounded and maimed, his defense (to avoid the death penalty) alleged his still-developing brain was manipulated by his older brother Tamerlan, who was killed in a police shootout. However, the jury rejected the defense's premise as convincing and sentenced the bomber to death.

The U.S. Supreme Court is still weighing in on the emerging science that indicates a juvenile's immature brain should be considered in the sentencing they receive pursuant to a conviction, even of a violent crime. In 2005, the court decided in *Roper v. Simmons* that the death penalty was unconstitutional for juveniles, a ruling which was determined should also apply to sentences of life without the possibility of parole for those who committed crimes as juveniles. The American Psychological Association agreed and published their position in support, based upon the following precepts:

"1) immaturity, that juveniles have an underdeveloped sense of responsibility which can result in ill-considered actions and decisions;

2) vulnerability, that juveniles are more susceptible to negative influences and peer pressure; and 3) changeability, that the character of juveniles is not as well-formed as that of an adult thereby giving juveniles greater potential for rehabilitation.

In summary, the brief presents research that is relevant to determining that given juveniles' diminished culpability and enhanced prospects for rehabilitation, a sentence of death in prison is inconsistent with principles of proportionality in criminal punishment"[28].

This case was followed by *Miller v. Alabama* in 2012, involving fourteen-year-old Evan Miller, sentenced to life without possibility of parole after he and another boy killed his neighbor during a robbery in 2003, then set the man's trailer on fire to destroy implicating evidence. The

Supreme Court found that this sentence violated his Eighth Amendment right to freedom from cruel and unusual punishment.

On the other hand, two law professors from prestigious institutions have agreed that while the science of immature healthy brains is compelling, "Current research cannot contribute usefully to legal decisions about individual adolescents and should not be used in criminal trials at the present time, except to provide general developmental information"[29].

Richard Bonnie of the University of Virginia School of Law and Elizabeth Scott of the Columbia University Law School agreed that the study of neuroscience as it relates to criminal behavior is relatively new, but argued as to how risky behavior that may occur in adolescence can evaporate in adulthood, giving credence to more compassionate sentencing and interventions. Bonnie and Scott also contend that extended incarceration of juveniles will not only be counterproductive but will increase recidivism. This is due in large part to prolonged exposure to other criminals in a confined environment where survival consumes everyday life. This social transference can increase the risk of a juvenile being consumed by a gang for survival, which will introduce them to a criminal culture that is hard to escape.

To further demonstrate the quagmire of issues involved with deciding how to prosecute and punish violent juvenile offenders, let us examine one final example, one which touches the extreme limit of explicable behavior.

By all accounts, Anissa Weier, Morgan Geyser, and Payton Leutner were typical small-town pre-teen girls. They had sleepovers, played with dolls, and talked on the phone with friends. Little did Leutner know that, over a period of months, her friends were conspiring to kill her. Their reason was not anger, or jealousy, or even boredom; rather, it was to satisfy the suggestions of a fictional character popularized by the internet.

Weier and Geyser had become enamored with the story of the Slender Man, a fabricated myth of a faceless man dressed in a suit with tentacles growing out of his back, who supposedly wanders forests looking for children. They became obsessed with the idea of becoming his "proxies", leaving home and living in his secluded mansion in the northern Wisconsin woods, supposedly located some five hours away by car from their homes.

In order to achieve this dream, they would have to kill Leutner. Originally, they planned to kill their friend during a sleepover in May 2014, but tabled that plan until the next day when, during a game of hide-and-seek in a nearby wooded area, Geyser stabbed Leutner nineteen times while Weier cheered her on[30]. Geyser would later tell the court, "Anissa told her to lie down so she wouldn't lose blood so quickly, and told her to be quiet, and we left"[31].

Miraculously, Leutner lived, but while originally there was a drive to prosecute the girls as adults, it was later learned that Geyser was delusional from schizophrenia and psychotic spectrum disorder. She pleaded guilty to first degree intentional homicide, but rather than being sent to prison, she was sentenced to forty years in a mental institution. Weier had pleaded guilty the previous December to being party to an attempted second-degree intentional homicide and was sentenced to twenty-five years in a psychiatric hospital. Both also spent more than three years in a juvenile detention center.

MEDICATIONS

It's the American dictum—if you want a medical issue fixed fast, medicate it.

There is a growing body of evidence that links an increase in frequency of psychiatric medications given to children and the rise of otherwise inexplicable violent crime. Attention Deficit Hyperactivity Disorder (ADHD), anxiety, and depression are among the most common medical diagnoses for children. Medications such as Ritalin, Paxil, Prozac, Luvox, and Zoloft are now seen by physicians as a logical means to quell these behaviors and symptoms. But in doing so they may have inadvertently, despite full knowledge of the potential side effects, created killers.

Physicians rarely look at the big picture—things like home life, nutrition, etc.—when prescribing medication. Instead, the focus is on whatever symptoms the child is presenting with. Medication, in these cases, is therefore seen as expedient and (hopefully) effective. Then, after receiving their medication, the children are returned to whatever environment is causing their symptoms—now as medicated "zombies".

Overmedication of children is not only counterproductive, it is harmful both to them and possibly the community at large. Selective Serotonin Reuptake Inhibitors (SSRIs) such as Celexa, Prozac, and Zoloft have been shown to increase suicidal tendencies, especially during withdrawal from the drug[32]. For this reason, the FDA has only granted approval for Prozac and Lexapro to be used for treating depression in children. Likewise, only Prozac, Zoloft and Luvox are approved for treating children and adolescents with obsessive compulsive disorder[33]. Of note, it wasn't until 2004 that the FDA issued a public warning as to the risk of suicidal thoughts and behavior in children on anti-depressants. Interestingly, the prescribing of antidepressants increased nearly four hundred percent between 1988 and 2008,[34] which incidentally coincides with the exponential increase of school related shootings in the United States during that period.

Consider the following attacks by juveniles who were either known or suspected to have been prescribed anti-depressants:

1988: James Wilson, 19, shot and killed two elementary school children and wounded seven others as well as two teachers at an elementary school in Greenwood, South Carolina. He had been prescribed Xanax, Valium, Thorazine and Haldol since he was fourteen years old[35].

1998: Kip Kinkel, 14, shot and killed his parents, and then went to Thurston High School, Springfield, Oregon, killing two and wounding twenty-two. He was reportedly prescribed Prozac and Ritalin and had been attending "anger management" classes[36].

1999: Eric Harris, 18, one of the two teens responsible for the Columbine High School massacre, was taking Luvox[37].

2005: Jeff Weise, 16, killed his grandfather and companion then went to Red Lake Senior High School in Minnesota where he killed seven, including himself. Reportedly, his dose of Prozac had just been increased to 60 mg daily[38].

2007: Cho Seung-Hui, 23, killed thirty-two people and himself at Virginia Tech University. The deeply disturbed young man had been prescribed Prozac but at the time of his autopsy no drugs were found in his system[39].

2012: Adam Lanza, 20, the infamous Sandy Hook Elementary School shooter in Connecticut, killed twenty children and six adults on a shooting rampage that included the murder of his mother and himself. Lanza had been prescribed the anti-depressant Lexapro; when he appeared to have an adverse reaction to that, he was prescribed Celexa.

These are the biggest mass murders potentially linked to SSRIs as a contributing factor (these incidents do not include the numerous isolated cases of homicide/suicide which cite a potential influence of SSRIs as a contributing factor). As with any homicidal act discussed in this book, the totality of the individual's state of mind, medications, and environment must be considered. When discussing medications, especially psychoactive medication, it must be remembered that their prescription is a direct result of an underlying psychiatric disorder.

Regardless, physicians must be held to their Hippocratic oath to do no harm and treat the entire patient, not just the symptoms. This means taking into account environment, nutrition, habits, triggers, and coping mechanisms. This last item in particular; as we will see when discussing the twin topics of bullying and facing adversity, the importance of coping and support mechanisms cannot be overstated. Combine poor coping mechanisms with SSRIs, and you might just have a recipe for disaster.

SCHOOL ENVIRONMENT

Schools should be a sanctuary for children, not only for their educational but their social development. From around the age of five or six years old, a child's school experience will have a profound impact on their emotional and physical development. Schools are a place where a teen's identity and reputation can be made or broken, and their experiences in school can have short- and long-term positive and negative effects, which in turn can strengthen or weaken them well into adulthood. As we have seen with the majority of mass school shootings, violent incidents can result from a breakdown in the maintenance of the sanctuary for students, some of whom feel compelled to use violence as their form of conflict resolution.

In a generation that already has challenges coping with adversity and perhaps even less support at home than ever before, the school environment can be daunting. Bullying is not a new phenomenon; it has been an unfortunate element of growing up for teens since there have been children in close proximity to one another. It's almost Darwinian in its elemental nature: the strong preying on the weak. The question therefore becomes, what has changed in the past twenty years that has sparked an exponential increase in children responding to bullying by shooting multiple classmates? We haven't adequately figured out the answer to that yet, but there are more than a few likely culprits. For example, social media (or antisocial media, as I like to call it) has had a profound impact on adolescent self-esteem, causing teen angst to be seen by millions of viewers.

A child is like a pressure cooker that accepts and internalizes days, weeks, or even years of abuse online—whether because of their looks, their weight, personal quirks, handicaps, or anything an insensitive classmate can latch onto. Eventually that pressure comes out, in often violent or self-destructive forms—since 1968, the teen suicide rate has increased by a third[40].

Even as recently as May 2018, Dimitrios Pagourtzis, 17, who shot and killed ten and wounded another ten at Santa Fe High School in Texas, intended to commit suicide after his shooting rampage. It was later revealed that one possible motive for his actions was that a girl, whom he ultimately murdered, had previously humiliated him, thus potentially acting as the catalyst for turning his simmering mental state into boiling action.

What is especially noteworthy is the comment made by Pagourtzis' defense attorney shortly after the tragedy, regarding how his client was being bullied by one of his football coaches. This allegation of "teacher-on student" bullying[41] was borne out by a student who said, "Coach would say that he stunk, smelled like crap"[42]. These are words a troubled teen, one who was likely walking through crowded halls feeling virtually invisible, with low self-esteem, did not need to hear—especially from someone who was supposed to be a caring school official. In the context of athletics, some may perceive this as attempting to "toughen" a kid up, but there are ways to do this without resorting to personal insults. Even the military has gotten away from the kinds of personal insults and hazing made famous in the opening scene of the film *Full Metal Jacket*.

There are definite strategies that can be implemented to discipline or "toughen" up a student, with yelling and insults being among the least effective. Consider the home lives some of the more "difficult" students come from, which may involve profound emotional and/ or physical abuse, whether to themselves, their mothers, or their siblings. My wife, a veteran special education teacher, related a story of one middle school student who had come to school the day after experiencing a night of domestic violence, where his drunken father had beat his mother. The child was forced to retreat to his bedroom and was up all night, fearfully listening to the barrage of insults and abuse. The next day, he had to walk five miles to school because he missed the bus. When he arrived at school late, he was met by a secretary who harangued him for being late without a parent available to sign him in. After enduring *that*, he went to his second period class, which was at that time taking a test, and innocently told his teacher he didn't have a pencil. Rather than sense something was wrong with the student and accommodating him with something as simple as a pencil, the teacher berated him for being late and not prepared. In response, the student began flipping desks over, causing officials to clear the room and call police. The police found out his story, which was conveyed to school officials. The student was not reprimanded and was given breakfast and allowed to calm down, speak to a counselor and return to class.

Why are incidents like this allowed to reach this point? Teacher bullying occurs more frequently than schools want to admit, and rarely is there any accountability or even training offered to prevent it. Though none would ever admit it, there *are* teachers who enjoy abusing their power just for the sake of demonstrating that they have it. It must be remembered that many at-risk teens come from environments not dissimilar from this student. Coming from homes where verbal and physical abuse are the norm, teachers yelling at, intimidating and insulting a student under the guise of discipline not only has little beneficial effect, it will ultimately add to an already strained and struggling psyche.

And, of course, there is peer bullying. Rarely do you see the face-to-face bullying of bygone generations; that was bad enough, but at least there was a confined level of exposure to the embarrassment. No longer: cyber bullying now opens a troubled child's wounds to the entire world, providing millions of people with the opportunity to learn about their human failings. You might say try ignoring it, but this is virtually impossible for teens; the harassment becomes a festering wound on the screen of their phone, or laptop. They become isolated on their own tormented digital island with the whole world laughing at them.

Efforts have been made to quell this aspect of adolescence through educational programs and zero tolerance policies in schools. Yet despite these efforts, there will always be offensive comments exchanged between adolescents. What is needed to truly complement anti-bullying strategies is to provide coping strategies for the child who is being "bullied". Reprimanding the "bully" without teaching their victim coping skills is counter-productive. Throughout life, there will always be people who will be mean to others. It is an unpleasant yet unavoidable fact of life. The proper, healthy response is to deal with this in a constructive fashion, not through violence or vengeance.

In the majority of school shootings, we see bullying emerge as one of the common denominators. There still isn't a logical explanation why an emotionally troubled juvenile is capable of walking into a school and start indiscriminately shooting students and teachers. But there is a totality of circumstances—warning signs that either are not noticed or go ignored. It is only in retrospect, when the media arrives at these tragedies, that we see the facts start to add up: "He was a quiet kid who kept to himself," we hear. "He was a loner."

Or even worse: "I always thought he'd be the one to bring a gun to school."

NEGATIVE RELATIONSHIP EXPERIENCE

When it comes to romances, love is an emotion difficult to quantify at any age, especially when it is a teen's first experience with that most elusive of mind states. Often times their experiences are more akin to the pangs of infatuation, but in their underdeveloped minds they feel that this is the love of their life—a love for eternity. These emotions are especially profound among children where love and affection are absent at home.

So what happens when these relationships end? The teen may feel as if their world has come to an end. In the deepest depths of depression, some of these more vulnerable teens may turn to suicide, as they feel they no longer have anything to live for, no future of a loving relationship where they are cared for, or can care for another. Others take it to the opposite extreme and decide to kill their former partner, feeling if they can't have them, no one can—tragedies in their own right, which can also turn into murder-suicides, as in the case of seventeen-year-old Austin Rollins. In March 2018, Rollins brought a handgun to his high school in Maryland and shot and killed his sixteen-year-old former girlfriend, whom he had recently broken up with. Before a school resource officer could intervene, Rollins turned the gun on himself[43].

Among the worst incidents I've ever reported on during my time as a crime reporter was the murder of a star high school basketball player by her equally skilled former boyfriend.

Eighteen-year-old Brooke Spencer had just finished another successful season for Gallup High School's female basketball team, a perennial New Mexico powerhouse. Colleges had already been scouting her not only to play basketball but also softball. Her graduation in May 2006 brought with it the conundrum of which college to go to. In June, she broke up with long-time boyfriend, Phillip Notah, 18. The couple was known to have had a tumultuous relationship.

On the night of June 5, 2006, Notah and Spencer had gotten together and were sitting in his car outside her house on the Navajo reservation. After some two hours they began to argue outside the car about her plans to go to college, which would invariably separate them, when Notah took out a knife and drove it into Spencer's chest. She stumbled into her house as Notah drove away, and was able to tell her mother what had happened. Spencer would be flown to a Phoenix area hospital where she would soon die of her injuries. Notah was taken into custody later that night; resisting arrest, police were forced to subdue him with a Taser. He would eventually plead guilty to second degree murder and would be sentenced to fifteen years in a federal prison (as the homicide occurred on the Navajo Reservation[44]).

It would eventually emerge (from conversations I had with Spencer's mother) that her daughter's relationship with Notah was fraught with arguments and threats, including him threatening to kill himself if she broke up with him. On the night of her death, Spencer was reluctant to go out with Notah who had texted her saying he wanted to see her. He had expressed his dissatisfaction with her going to college before. Almost prophetically, she texted him back, "You're just going to pull out another knife," if they got together.

In this brutal incident, we see another complicating factor in teen violence: understanding, avoiding, and combatting domestic violence. There is a gross misperception that domestic violence only pertains to married couples or adults. As Spencer found out and as her mother continues to advocate, both teen girls and boys need to be aware of the signs, not only physical but emotional abuse, as either one can lead to catastrophe if not checked immediately.

Then there are the overly possessive relationships seen where a partner will resort to extremes to protect the relationship from interlopers, whether real or perceived. This played out in the form of yet one more teen homicide on the streets of Chicago in 2014, when one fourteen-year-old girl fatally shot another girl of the same age on a Southside street over a Facebook feud involving a boy. According to Chicago Police Superintendent Garry McCarthy: "This was a fistfight that turned to a murder with the introduction of a firearm"[45].

Going back to our earlier discussion of environment the interconnectedness of these factors in understanding teen violence, other individuals were arrested with the girl, including a twenty-four-year-old relative. What kind of environment must she have been living in that helped fuel this kind of response?

SUBSTANCE ABUSE

In discussing why teens kill, we would be remiss if we did not include those homicides committed to feed substance abuse habits or narcotic enterprises.

For more than thirty years, drug violence among teens has resulted in a swathe of blood and human destruction across the American landscape. According to the National Council on Alcoholism and Drug Dependence, four of every five teens in state juvenile justice systems are under the influence of alcohol or drugs while committing their crimes, test positive for drugs, are arrested for committing an alcohol or drug offense, admit to having substance abuse and addiction problems, or share some combination of these characteristics. A report listed that, in a single year, 1.9 million of the 2.4 million juvenile arrests recorded in America had substance abuse and addiction issues, yet only 68,600 of those juveniles received substance abuse treatment[46]. (This report did not provide a year for this data but rest assured the annual fluctuation is not significantly different.)

Perhaps the most disturbing crime I had the misfortune to report on dealt with the murder of a beloved Roman Catholic nun in the remote reservation community of Navajo, New Mexico. Amid the red rock mesas and pinon trees, sixty-four-year-old Sister Marguerite Bartz of the Order of the Sisters of the Blessed Sacrament dedicated herself to working with the poor on the Navajo Reservation. She lived in a modest mobile home on the grounds of St. Berard Mission.

On the night after Halloween 2009, a real horror story unfolded.

A local teenager, eighteen-year-old Reehahlio Carroll broke into the nun's home, intending to steal whatever he could get his hands on to fuel his substance abuse. According to the FBI, Carroll broke a window to gain access to Sister Bartz's mobile home, rummaging through drawers and cabinets searching for cash and items of value that he could sell for cash or trade for drugs or alcohol. Carroll found a flashlight in one of the rooms that he used for illumination as he continued searching for items to steal. When Carroll encountered Sister Bartz in one of the bedrooms, she attempted to defend herself by hitting him with a slipper. He then brutally battered the nun, beating her repeatedly with the flashlight and then, in an attempt to silence her, strangling her with a T-shirt. The pathologist who performed the autopsy concluded that the cause of death was multiple blunt force head trauma and ligature strangulation[47]. Carroll would ultimately pay for his selfish act of depravity by being sentenced to forty years in federal prison.

SUGGESTIONS AND STRATEGIES

The causative factors of teen violence are complex, and rarely act in exclusion of each other. It cannot be stressed enough that early identification and intervention are essential to help children avoid potentially destructive paths, for no other reason than they don't see any another option.

So, what are the difficulties inhibiting early identification and action? Oftentimes, the parents are to blame, either reluctant to admit their child has a "problem" or neglectful in getting them care they need. Other times, the parents—and the environment they've created—are the problem, turning what should be the first line of defense into the threat itself.

We have also seen, time and time again, the failings of child protective services. These shortcomings are not only institutional, due to flaws inherent in the system, but are also due to the overwhelming caseloads placed on woefully under supported social workers. These problems combine to allow warning signs to fall through the cracks, as bureaucratic policies neglect the seriousness of a child's environment.

Beyond repairing the policies themselves, there needs to be a greater emphasis on looking into behavioral warning signs; i.e., what is and isn't normal behavior for a child. From this starting point, the contributing factors to the aberrant behavior must be identified by trained professionals, whether at school or through social services. Medication is not always the answer. Each child's behavior must be examined in its totality, looking for cause and effect. If they are acting a certain way, why?

- Are they developmentally healthy? Is the brain working the way it should be, given the individual's age?
- Are there behavioral issues?
- Is the home environment stable?
- Do they abuse drugs/alcohol?
- Are they suffering post-traumatic stress disorder? If so, why? Is it secondary to being involved in, witnessing, or knowing someone who was in a traumatic incident?
- Are they suffering the side effects of a traumatic brain injury?

These are just some starting points. Intervention should be holistic in nature, and address the child, their family, home and school environment.

Interventions can include, but should not be limited to:

- Individual and group counseling
- Providing proper nutrition
- Appropriate prescription/monitoring/compliance of medication
- Family coaching
- Teaching conflict resolution techniques
- Substance abuse counseling
- Removal from a deleterious family environment (where necessary)
- Providing access to resources

CONCLUSION

Based on the information presented in this chapter, we can safely say there appears not to be a singular explanation for youth violence. Teen violence can't be put in a box and neatly tied up with a bow, providing a clean, simple package for advocates and politicians to point to and say this or that factor "caused" a particular tragedy. The causes of violent acts must be looked at in their totality, which can make interventions and solutions hard to find. This is one reason why early identification of a "problem" for at-risk children and subsequent intervention is crucial. A proverbial ticking time bomb may have already experienced repeated incidents, needing only one last push to send them towards violence.

Yale University researcher David Katz sums up the issue by saying there is a "confluence of trends"[48]: "Recent studies highlight the rising prevalence of both depression and opioid abuse in the U.S. Combine these with yet another feature of American life—the ubiquity of guns—and there is a potent and ominous mix"[49].

According to Bennett, DiIulio, and Walters, authors of the book *Body Count: Moral Poverty and How to win America's War Against Crime and Drugs*, when a child is born into a life devoid of loving, capable, responsible adults who teach right from wrong, they grow up without any kind of moral compass. Tens of thousands of children are exposed to the same risk factors relating to criminal behavior and violence, but not all become "super predators."

In future chapters, we will discuss remedies to this type of moral poverty, but in short the absence of a moral compass is the result of this confluence of factors, all of which have a variable effect on an individual's proclivity towards violent crime. These factors combine to create the teen's environment and dictate the nature of their day-to-day life, and any prevention plan that involves returning a child to the very cauldron that created his violent behavior is one that only invites future violence.

CHAPTER 3
THE GANG LIFE

"Even gang members imagine a future that doesn't include gangs."
—GREG BOYLE

THE 2016 SCHOOL year had just begun at Brentwood Ross High School in Suffolk County Long Island, some forty-five minutes east of New York City. Tuesday, September 13 was a balmy seventy-seven degrees with a light breeze. Summer was hanging on for a few more weeks, with daylight still lingering until well after 7:00 PM, when life-long best friends Nisa Mickens and Kayla Cuevas, 16, went for a walk in their neighborhood of tree-lined streets and manicured front lawns. On Stahley Street, just outside the gate of Loretta Park Elementary School, a car full of young men pulled over and stopped the girls less than an hour into their walk, who immediately knew something terrible was unfolding.

In the months leading up to the fateful encounter, Cuevas was involved in a series of disputes with members of the local Sailors clique of the notorious gang, MS-13. Approximately one week prior to this incident, these disputes escalated when Cuevas and several friends were involved in an altercation with MS-13 members at their school. After that incident, the gang vowed to seek revenge against Cuevas and, on the evening of September 13, 2016, Selvin "Flash" Chavez, Alexi "Big Homie" Saenz, Jairo "Funny" Saenz, Enrique "Oso" Portillo , and other members of the Sailors Locos Salvatruchas Westside (Sailors) clique of MS-13 agreed to hunt for rival gang members to kill. They split off in different vehicles and drove around Brentwood looking for targets[1].

Chavez, Portillo, and two other juvenile MS-13 members who were riding together in one car, saw Cuevas and Mickens walking down Stahley Street. They recognized Cuevas and called "Big Homie" and "Funny", the leaders of the Sailors clique, who authorized them to kill the two girls. Chavez, the driver, pulled up close to the girls, then Portillo and the other gang members jumped out of the car and attacked them with baseball bats and a machete, striking the girls numerous times in the head and body. After finishing the attack, Portillo and the others got back into the car and Chavez drove them away[2].

The attack was rapid and brutal. There is indication that Mickens gallantly attempted to fight off the attackers, protecting her friend from being taken by the gang members and giving her time to flee for her life through adjoining suburban yards[3]. When the brutal assault against Mickens was over, she lay in the street with multiple blunt force trauma and slashes to her head and face, which left her unrecognizable.

Mickens' body was found on the side of the road by a passing motorist about 8:30 PM. She was supposed to turn sixteen the next day, but rather than celebrate a landmark occasion in any girl's life, Mickens' parents, who were preparing for their daughter's party back home, received the news that every parent dreads.

It wouldn't be until the next day that the brutally beaten and slashed body of Cuevas, who made it into the nearby woods just a block from her own house, would be discovered brutalized in the same fashion as her best friend.

What has escaped in-depth analysis in the discussion of this horrendous attack was how the screams of two teenage girls being brutally chased and murdered in a residential neighborhood, in daylight, went apparently unheard by people finishing their dinners or watching television in the nearby homes. It evokes memories of the 1964 Kitty Genovese incident that occurred in Kew Gardens, Queens, a short drive from Brentwood, where the twenty-eight-year-old woman was brutally stabbed outside her apartment and her screams for help went ignored. But Genovese was killed around 3 AM, in the depths of the early morning[4]; clearly, this case pointed to something more serious.

Following the murders of Mickens and Cuevas, a rash of MS-13 murders swept Long Island, a spree of violence which also included the uncovering of bodies murdered before the girls. In April 2017, for example, the bodies of four mutilated young men, all between the ages of sixteen and twenty, were found in a park in nearby Central Islip[5]. MS-13 introduced a regional crime wave the likes of which no one had ever seen before—but which was nevertheless not unheard of. MS-13 had been committing a string of homicides for nearly twenty years in nearby areas before the incident with Mickens and Cuevas.

It was the brutality of the crimes that sparked outrage and inspired Cuevas's mother, Evelyn Rodriguez, who had left the mean streets of the South Bronx for the seemingly safe suburban community of Brentwood, to become an advocate—not only for her daughter but for legislation and methods to suppress this transnational gang that has proliferated throughout dozens of communities in at least forty-two states, with some ten thousand members[6]. It was her hope that other parents would not have to experience her pain.

Rodriguez would also go on to hold the school district responsible for her daughter's death. "They let my daughter into that environment with no protection. They told me my daughter was safe and she wasn't," Rodriguez said in an interview[7]. In December 2017, Rodriguez filed a $110 million lawsuit against the Brentwood Union Free School District, claiming the district knew MS-13 gang members were harassing her daughter and threatened her life but did nothing about it[8].

In a macabre twist of fate, Rodriguez would later be killed at the very spot where her daughter was murdered. In September 2018, two years to the day of her daughter's murder, while preparing a candlelight vigil to commemorate her daughter's murder, Rodriguez was fatally struck by a vehicle. Police said Rodriguez got into an altercation with a woman driving a white 2016 Nissan Rogue over a memorial for the two girls that had been dismantled in front of a house on the block. The driver then ran her over, and she later died at a local hospital.

The parents of the victims in this incident have one small consolation. The killers of their children were arrested some six months later. But gang violence continues not only on Long Island but Chicago and other large and small cities across America. This is a dynamic that is not new to American society—each generation for more than one hundred and fifty years has had to identify and suppress violent crime. An unfortunate consequence of this history, and which was seen in the case on Long Island, is that the response is usually reactive to a specific crime, as in the case of Mickens and Cuevas, or a crime wave. There is little community-wide emphasis on preventing gang development and crime.

That is why, in this chapter, we will be looking at the causative factors, warning signs, and potential solutions to teenagers joining and committing gang violence.

AMERICA'S GANG HERITAGE

Gang violence in America is nothing new. Before there was MS-13, there were the Crips and Bloods, the Surenos, the Mexican Mafia and Latin Kings; before them there were the Whyo gang, the Bowery Boys, and the Dead Rabbits dating back to the early Irish immigrants.

Criminal gangs have been a subculture in the American narrative since the late 1700s, but it wasn't until the Irish diaspora of the early 1800s that the identity of gangs became more defined and even necessary for self-protection against overt acts of violent discrimination against immigrant groups. It can be argued that most gangs at the time did not emerge with a direct intent towards criminality, as opposed to self-defense and preservation against the dominant culture. Eventually, crimes of opportunity lent themselves to more aggressive abuse of their own people. A similar dynamic would also play out with succeeding racial and ethnic groups, who only later moved on the offensive to protect their "turf".

Irish gangs gave way to subsequent immigrants from China, Italy, and Jews from Eastern Europe, which gave way to Mexican and Russian immigrants, and so on. Just about every immigrant population that came to America to escape persecution and violence, or seek economic opportunities not realized in their home countries, were obligated to band together to retain cultural identity and show solidarity in an unfamiliar country.

Ironically, these immigrants were then (and still are) victimized by gangs of their own ethnic origin, with extortion to provide "protection" against established nativist criminal elements being among the most prevalent tactics. Failure to comply often led to damaged property, kidnapping, attack, or death. The romantic myth portrayed in the classic musical *West Side Story,* where the leader of the white gang the Jets falls in love with the sister of a Puerto Rican gang member in late 1950s New York. Entertaining the movie was, but dancing and prancing gang members could not be farther from the truth, especially in a time when there was growing antipathy and actual gang violence between these two groups.

The first immigrant gang in the U.S. to transcend their roots was the Italian Black Hand in New York. Not to be confused with the contemporary Mexican Mafia prison gang, this gang of Italian mobsters permeated throughout any locale where Italian immigrants settled. Whether it was the congested and tepid streets of Little Italy in downtown Manhattan or the coal mines of rural West Virginia, the Black Hand instilled fear in every immigrant family, demanding extortion and favors at the risk of certain and brutal death.

My own family history includes a tragic run-in with the Black Hand: as family lore has it, my great grandfather was murdered by the notorious gang. The circumstances are murky—they typically are in such cases—but there is suspicion that it involved a woman. Fortunately, my grandfather avoided this temptation and had a distinguished twenty-year career, retiring as a detective with the New York City Police Department. He followed in the proud tradition of Italian NYPD officers launched by Detective Giuseppe (Joe) Michael Pasquale Petrosino, born in 1860, who was the first Italian assigned to the NYPD in an effort to penetrate and dismantle the Black Hand, and effort which would ultimately cost Petrossino his life[9].

The lessons learned from Petrossino's actions over a century ago are still relevant today. He urged the Italian community to come forward to assist him and his fellow Italian detectives to fight the gang. The NYPD realized that forming an "Italian Squad" would be the most effective means of combating the gang due to the cultural and language particulars often required to investigate the cases and interview suspects and witnesses. Likewise, when dealing with MS-13 and its typically Central American victims, having officers with roots from that region can increase trust and help build a relationship with the community, especially in a time when immigration enforcement has forced many in this demographic into the shadows, reluctant to report crimes to law enforcement.

In fact, there are many similarities between the Italian Black Hand of the late 1800s and MS-13 today: the violent predatory practice of intimidating and controlling their own immigrant population through murder and extortion; the spread and growth of the gang concurrent with the migration pattern of the immigrant population; the proposal of immigration legislation to control entry or expulsion of gang members. And in the end, it has still come down to dogged police work to suppress the gang, though—then as now—little has been done in terms of prevention and protection of vulnerable immigrants. (MS-13 will be discussed in greater detail later on in this chapter, including its unique issues which led to their designation as the sole street gang to be classified a transnational criminal organization by the U.S. Treasury Department.)

Of course, not all gangs are immigrant-based. On the domestic level, gangs such as the Crips and Bloods emerged as a way to protect themselves from each other and those who would infringe on their "turf". Prison gangs form along racial and ethnic lines for self-preservation, which then spill over onto the streets once they are released, producing a dual-environment of criminality.

Yet despite the risk of death and long-term incarceration, the attraction of gangs is inescapable for thousands of vulnerable teens. And there's no easy fix—especially since the risk factors tied to gang enticement can be so overwhelming for the individual.

CURRENT GANG PRESENCE IN THE UNITED STATES

There are an estimated 1.4 million active gang members involved with more than 33,000 gangs in the United States[10]. This is a staggering number, albeit one that is very fluid based on arrests and recruiting data, of which the latter is impossible to detect. This is especially true when we consider the impact of more than 30,000 unaccompanied children entering the United States from Central America and the impact those numbers have on MS-13 recruitment and unreported victimization. (The murders of Mickens and Cuevas were actually an anomaly for MS-13, who typically murder other Central Americans.)

Teen involvement in gangs has been a driving force in the juvenile demographic's crime rates for decades. In a 2010 article written for

Psychology Today, Raychelle Cassada identifies 24,500 known youth gangs containing 772,500 youth members, which represents about seven percent of the U.S. teen population[11]. By 2012, that number had increased to over 30,000 known gangs with 850,000 members[12]. But perhaps the most concerning figure is the thirty-five percent increase in gang-related homicides in cities with over 100,000 inhabitants. The reasons behind these trends continue to be examined, with no coherent explanation yet having been found. The drug trade in these cities do form the foundation for the majority of violent crimes. But while the experts ponder these questions, the rate of teen gang membership continues to rise.

One statistic that deserves greater explanation is the reported decrease in age of young gang members. In 2011, thirty-five percent of gang members were under eighteen years of age, compared to fifty percent in 1996[13]. This number indicates that while there is a creeping increase in young gang members, as reported by Cassada, it also shows that after joining a gang, more teens are deciding to stay in. I regularly see these OGs (original gangsters) in my jail: men and women in their fifties and sixties, still proudly representing their gang.

Yet for all these figures, we're left with no definitive explanation for why these trends are increasing. Possibilities include the "revolving door" juvenile justice system, where compassion is mistaken for leniency; the vast quantities of cheap heroin and crystal meth flooding America's streets from Mexican drug trafficking organizations; the 2006 mortgage crisis, which hit minorities especially hard due to predatory lenders; the continued erosion of the family and domestic instability; and even the unaccompanied youth crisis mentioned earlier, which saw tens of thousands of children show up at the U.S.-Mexican border from gang-violence plagued El Salvador, Guatemala, and Honduras.

Take juvenile angst, drugs and alcohol, and an adolescent sense of invincibility, and mix in the knowledge that most of these children have little to look forward to beyond their teenage years, and you have a recipe for bloodletting—so much so that sixty percent of teen gang members are more likely to die from homicide. In New York City alone, there are an estimated three hundred youth gangs, whose members range in age from twelve to twenty[14]. These 'young guns' are responsible for forty percent of the city's shootings. "It's like belonging to an evil fraternity," Inspector Kevin Catalina, commander of the New York Police Department's gang division said in an interview. "A lot of it is driven by nothing: a dispute over a girl or a wrong look or a perceived slight"[15].

So what is the teenage attraction to this life of uncertainty, with no prospects other than jail or the grave? Understanding the reason why more than a million American teens are in gangs is a valuable step in implementing appropriate preventive and rehabilitative strategies.

GANG ATTRACTIONS

There are myriad reasons why young people join gangs. Of course, the oldest reason for joining stems from the factors we discussed previously: the threat of racial and ethnic ostracism/persecution, in turn creating the need for protection through unity of numbers. This is what unfolded on the streets of New York and Boston with the arriving Irish, Italian, and Jewish immigrants who were persecuted by the settled Americans who had preceded them. The refusal to welcome those different from them was itself a threat, one that was frequently acted out. Similar racial and ethnic responses were played out by Mexicans and Salvadorans in California, Puerto Ricans and Dominicans in New York, as well as African-Americans on both coasts.

Among teens, the most common reason for joining a gang is to fill a void, typically one created by a dysfunctional homelife or a family where there is a lack of parental presence, loving attention, and most importantly, moral guidance—the moral poverty Bennet and his colleagues describe[16].

Jamal Williams, a New York City gang member, says he joined a gang when he was just nine years old. "A crew to me is a family," he says. "They are going to be there for me like my parents was never there for me."[17]

Add to this milieu all the additional risk factors of poverty, substance abuse, and a constant exposure to criminal activity, and these children—many of whom join gangs in elementary school—don't have a chance. Another developmental element ostensibly obtained through gang affiliation is structure and discipline, however distorted it might be. Many gangs have an organizational structure with a hierarchy, rules, initiation rites, meetings, obligations, and dress code. While anti-social in nature and criminally based, it still provides a structure the child can follow, structure that they do not have in the chaos of their home.

Paradoxically, there are also occasions where a child will turn to gang membership for socialization. I had the opportunity to interview a former member of the violent Barrio Azteca gang out of El Paso, Texas. By his own admission, Antonio (whose real name has been withheld as he has been marked for death for turning against the gang) was raised "in a family with two loving parents who taught me right from wrong." This rules out filling an emotional void as his dominant reason for gang involvement.

No, in Antonio's case, he joined for excitement and the lure of easy money. He was raised in Anthony, Texas, a small and poor farming village west of El Paso. "I wanted the houses, cars, and girls," he told me, things he knew he couldn't obtain legally in the small town. He joined the Barrio Azteca and quickly became a successful "earner," running his own drug operation and eventually controlling part of El Paso's drug trade.

That is, until he was arrested on an assault charge. Whether it was an epiphany as to how he wasted his life or an opportunity to save his own skin—likely a combination of the two—Antonio decided to cooperate with federal authorities, which eventually led to the arrest of multiple gang members. This earned him a lifelong "Green Light", or kill order. Just one more ignominious end a gang member can expect.

This brings me to the other reason for gang attraction among teens: income potential. Given the typically depressed socio-economic conditions gang members emerge from, the prospect of fast money to buy material things is difficult to overcome. They don't reconcile the risk-benefit relationship between their illegal activities and legitimate methods of earning money. Without wishing to justify this behavior, but for many of us who haven't been in their shoes: for a fifteen-year-old, living in a slum, not knowing where their next meal is coming from (if it ever comes at all), wearing worn and faded clothes, seeing nothing but limited and low-paying jobs that will essentially keep them in the same environment…the prospect of making the kinds of money seen by gang members, despite knowing the consequences, is overwhelming.

While there is as yet no unified theory of teenage gang attraction, it cannot be doubted that poverty is a key driver. One disadvantage of poverty is low self-esteem—gang affiliation gives a teen the sense of belonging to something greater than themselves. They see the respect, albeit typically due to fear, that gang members garner in their neighborhoods. For many adolescents, this may be the first and only time they'll feel respected and accepted. The consequences of disrespecting them, whether verbally or just through body language, will typically see a violent response from the teen looking to protect the respect they fear to lose.

This fact accounts for one of the biggest failures of our society. Although President George W. Bush advocated "No child left behind" in his educational initiatives, the truth is millions are left behind both socially and developmentally. We have spawned generations of invisible children, left on their own and to their own devices, despite the billions of dollars spent on failed government programs. Of course, countless children can and do avoid a life of crime, even while growing up in these environments; it's not a one to one ratio. In fact, there is much that can be learned from these children and applied to gang prevention programs. But sometimes it's hard to say no, especially when recruitment is also based on peer pressure and intimidation.

Which brings us to the next reason for teen gang enrolment: threats and coercion. When gangs recruit new members, there is typically a mutual sales pitch regarding what each party can offer the other. Is it protection? Income potential for both? Additional strength in numbers? The list is long, but one thing is for sure: sometimes teens are given an offer they can't refuse.

One tactic used by MS-13 targets immigrant children recently arrived in the U.S. Given their known influence back in Central America, they can threaten a child into joining by telling them that failure to do so will lead to their family back home being killed. Since the children know full well this is a credible threat, they join the gang.

It should be mentioned that these types of tactics aren't always necessary; membership can also be voluntary, as a recently arrived immigrant will typically be looking for some sense of assimilation and protection in their new environment.

GANGS IN SCHOOLS

Whatever the reason and method for recruitment, the unfortunate truth is that schools are the central repository for prospective members of any gang. "[MS-13] gets them in school," said Evelyn Rodriguez[18]. In December 2016, three seventeen-year-old students were arrested for attempting to recruit students into MS-13 at Manassas High School in Virginia, another MS-13 stronghold[19].

Of course, school recruiting is not just an MS-13 tactic; it happens every day with most gangs across the country. A prime example of this involved a father and daughter pair in Fairfax, Virginia. The daughter, at the behest of her own father, was recruiting students to join the Elm Street Piru Bloods[20]. This is why it is imperative that school officials be aware of the warning signs, not only of gang presence but recruitment and to closely monitor the dress and behavior of parents in and around their schools.

Ignorance of or ambivalence towards an emerging or existing gang presence in a school risks bringing the violence of the streets to the halls of the school. Far removed from the gang-infested urban centers is Spencer, Oklahoma, a suburb of Oklahoma City, with a population of less than five thousand people, predominately African-American and low-income. Remarkably, it is a hotbed for animosity between the Crips and Bloods.

In 2013, this tension exploded onto the grounds of Star Spencer High School. Officials said DonShea Brown had transferred to the school from a reported Bloods part of town, coming to Star Spencer High School which is in Crips controlled territory. Apparently, Brown was not a gang member, but members of his family were reputed to have been Bloods. Words were exchanged and Brown was jumped by a group of Crips, which resulted in a response from his Bloods relatives[21].

This is a prime example of the far-reaching influence of gangs on America's schools—an incident that highlights not so much a moral poverty but moral decay. Another incident occurred during a massive gang fight in the halls of Gallatin High School in Gallatin, Tennessee, a small city of less than thirty-five thousand people. In February 2017, fists started flying between gang members at the school. When the school resource officer tried to break up the fight, she was either pushed or tripped by someone and fell to the ground. Another teacher reported being cursed at and slapped in the face by a fourteen-year-old female student, who then slapped the assistant principal in the face as he escorted her to the office. In the end, a student was charged with assault and disorderly conduct for punching the assistant principal in the eye[22].

Unfortunately, many schools choose to ignore the fact they have a gang problem, which only allows the problem to proliferate under their noses. The presence of school resources officers and the importance of training teachers to recognize the warning signs of gangs are valuable first steps but it is ultimately up to the school administrators to establish uncompromising policies and work closely with law enforcement to protect the children in their charge. More school districts should follow the example of the Dallas Independent School District, which not only recognizes there are gangs in their schools but aggressively addresses the issue through a designated gang unit in the school district police department. The program model includes prevention, intervention, and enforcement strategies, the purpose of which is to increase awareness and to provide every educator and parent in Dallas ISD with a working knowledge of how gangs affect schools and communities.

One fact is for sure, ignoring gangs in schools will not make them go away. Ignorance is not bliss; it is deadly. Gangs will only become more emboldened in environments that do nothing to inhibit their activities.

GANGS: A BRIEF PRIMER

Not all gangs are the same. Different gangs have different origins, different criminal business models, identifiers, and initiation rites. For this and many other reasons, even defining what a gang or gang member is can be complicated, especially when considering the issue of free speech.

People are often shocked to hear that being in a gang is not, in itself, technically illegal—it is the acts they perpetrate, not their membership, that can land an individual in jail. If someone is brazen enough to walk through a particular neighborhood with their "colors" or tattoos on full display, that is their right. In Albuquerque, for example, itself a hotbed for the Bandidos outlaw motorcycle gang (or OMG, discussed later in this chapter), it is not uncommon to see members riding their bikes along Interstate 40 or Interstate 25 wearing their black leather with the distinctive red and gold patch on the back. The Bandidos are one of the most violent gangs in the U.S., yet they defy law enforcement and challenge rivals with the brazen flashing of their patch—all completely legally. This has resulted in violent eruptions not only in Albuquerque but in other parts of the Southwest, including the notorious 2015 Twin Peaks Restaurant shootout in Waco, Texas against the Cossacks OMG that left seven Cossacks dead.

So, what defines a gang? Among the criteria used by law enforcement to verify the establishment of a gang are:

1. A name for the gang as designated by its membership. Note that gangs can be established and recognized by law enforcement with as few as three to five members.

2. Commission of crimes together, in the name of the gang, or for the furtherance of the gang's goals.

3. Common identifiers such as colors, attire, accessories, tattoos, and graffiti.

4. Claims made to a specific geographic territory. There is rarely any ambiguity, since the gang will typically mark their territory with distinctive graffiti or "tags".

5. Self-admission. Most gang members, especially young, lower-level members, will unhesitatingly pronounce their gang membership out of pride and an arrogance towards authority.

Within this criteria are a number of subcategories, which bring with them additional identifying features.

Street Gangs

The most basic and common gang designation is that of a **street gang.** These are typically created along geographic or racial/ethnic lines. This is typically the starting point for most teen gang members. They see the daily operations and perks of gang life without fully weighing the risks, or they may be enticed to join by a family member or friend. In urban settings where gangs may control an entire apartment complex or neighborhood, resistance is daunting. Either way, membership is easily accessible and always within reach.

Most street gangs start with a few teens who, whatever their motivations and depending on their brutality and drug trafficking expertise, are able to proliferate in their region. This can then spread nationally or, in a few cases, even internationally. Street gangs are heavily involved to varying degrees in drug trafficking, whether that means controlling street corners in a section of a community or major interstate trafficking.

Other than a handful of street gangs, the majority do not have a sophisticated hierarchy and are instead loosely organized with a nondescript criminal business model. They may violently control a segment of the drug trade in their community but have no criminal reach beyond their home turf. This does not make them any less of a public safety threat; in fact, a lack of hierarchy, in which murders may have to be sanctioned before being carried out, can contribute to more spontaneous violence among impulsive teens.

The following is a list of the largest and most sophisticated street gangs in the United States. (This is in alphabetical order and does not reflect their level of power in the United States):

1. Bloods

2. Crips

3. Florencia 13

4. Gangster Disciples

5. Latin Kings (Almighty Latin King and Queen Nation)-

6. MS-13

7. Nortenos

8. Surenos

9. Vice Lords (Almighty Vice Lord Nation)

10. 18th Street

MS-13 AND THE UNACCOMPANIED MINOR CRISIS

MS-13 has received widespread national attention since the Cuevas-Mickens murders, garnering visits by President Donald Trump and U.S. Attorney General Jeff Sessions to the highly-impacted area of Long Island. Rather than discuss the gang's history and past bad acts, which are more than abundantly documented, let us concentrate on why and how this gang has at its disposal a seemingly endless recruiting pool as a result of U.S. immigration policy and what this means to teens hoping to escape the same threats from their home countries in Central America.

MS-13 is said to be run by a committee of inmates in El Salvador's prison system and administered through a series of regional structures called programs. A program can oversee multiple cliques, or the local franchises of the gang. There are more than one hundred cliques in over forty states throughout the U.S. Many cliques of the same name are found in multiple cities which can further complicate criminal investigation.

The unaccompanied minor crisis that began in 2013 and which brought more than three hundred thousand minors from Central America to the U.S. has created a boom for MS-13 in the form of recruits, as well as potential victims who thought they had escaped the violence by coming to the U.S. According to Immigration and Customs Enforcement, thirty percent of MS-13 members arrested in recent years are unaccompanied alien children, or UACs.

A 2015 Texas Department of Public Safety report said that the influx of UACs into the state, particularly in the Houston metro area, has had a direct influence on gang violence, causing the agency to elevate MS-13 from a Tier 2 to a Tier 1 gang. (Tier designation is based on numerous factors including size, level of violence, transnational criminal activity, prevalence throughout the area, juvenile membership, and threat to law enforcement.) The report says that since 2011, the number of MS-13 members encountered by U.S. Border Patrol has increased each year, accelerating in 2014 and coinciding with increased illegal migration from Central America during the same period.

While the U.S. Department of Health and Human Services' Office of Refugee Resettlement (ORR) has attempted to place these vulnerable children—traumatized by the conditions they saw in Central America even before embarking on a treacherous, two thousand-mile journey—there is only a cursory evaluation of the home life the child is to be placed in, and even less in terms of follow-up. ORR also refuses to notify schools and local social agencies, citing protection of the child's privacy, creating an overwhelming burden on already limited resources without doing the child any good.

In 2015, a whistleblower made the startling revelation to members of Congress that 3,400 sponsors out of the 29,000 listed in the UAC database had criminal convictions, including re-entry after deportation, DUI, burglary, distribution of narcotics, domestic violence, homicide, child molestation, and sexual assault[23]. From firsthand observations, we know that the majority of these children are not compliant with the provisions of their placement, and neither they or their sponsors are being held accountable. There are even cases where a UAC is suspected of committing a crime, but is not at the listed residence when police arrive to interview them. In short, the policy is a mess and very little is being done to rectify it, placing not only the UACs but the communities they live in in peril.

A former school administrator in the Amityville School District (hometown of the Amityville Horror) commented on the pressure cooker environments UACs are placed in, which overwhelms understaffed school districts: "Take a thirteen-year-old who isn't an English speaker. Unless he's so bright, and unless his family life at home is incredibly structured, there's no way he's getting through high school." He went on to say, "Fear, at a certain point, becomes anger. You can see it building up."[24].

Not coincidentally, the rate of MS-13 connected homicides increased exponentially on Long Island between 2014 and 2017, a three-year span in which UACs continued to flood the New York City suburb. During this time, there were at least twenty-five MS-13 related homicides[25] with bodies being unearthed from clandestine graves in relatively tranquil communities that were not familiar with this level of violence.

While there have been dozens of mass apprehensions of MS-13 suspects, what is not reported is how the UAC situation allows the gang to backfill what they lose to arrests. A frustrated Boston Police officer recently told me that even as they arrest gang members, more appear to be popping up with the new waves of placed UACs in Suffolk County, Massachusetts. In order to significantly suppress MS-13, there needs to be a more coherent definition of UACs and a determination on whether they fall under the actual law that addresses trafficked children. UACs can no longer be placed with sponsors who are in the U.S. illegally, and ORR needs to better prepare communities for any significant influx of these children in order for appropriate resources to be provided. Until then, MS-13 will continue to flourish in the U.S.

Crews

There is a gang subset called a **crew** which is typically underestimated—until they grow and commit violent crimes, that is. Crews may be a handful of bored and incorrigible teens who lack the organization and numbers of a sophisticated gang, and as such usually starts off as more of a public nuisance—a group of delinquents. Early activities are usually spontaneous and include acts of vandalism, such as breaking store windows or graffiti.

When little is done to quell this behavior, they become emboldened. Lip service paid by city officials and law enforcement, claiming that the actions of crews are those of a bunch of "wannabees" can be taken as a challenge by a rebellious teen group. Perceiving that they are not being taken seriously and with no hierarchy in place, their behavior becomes erratic and increasingly more violent. Add to that the problem of substance abuse and violence will eventually emerge. For this reason, crews should never be underestimated and should be suppressed as soon as they emerge.

Take, for example, the Get Hard Crew in Albuquerque, a crew which started at a local high school and quickly spread. The group started inauspiciously enough as a public nuisance, with "GHC" found spray painted on walls and doors around the city. Their activities rapidly graduated to violence, as Albuquerque police pinned a multitude of more serious crimes to GHC that included car theft, robberies, burglaries, shootings and violent crimes[26]. Five juveniles suspected of being part of GHC were pursued after allegedly beating a man and stealing his car at gunpoint in mid-October 2016, leading law enforcement on a high-speed chase that ended in a violent collision with an off-duty APD officer[27]. Later that year, GHC graduated into the realm of homicide when forty-seven-year-old Hector Aguirre was run over by GHC members Daniel Sandoval and Dominic Jiminez, both nineteen years old, with Aguirre's own work truck while he was working a job at a home in northwest Albuquerque. Also charged in the crime were Xavier Montoya, 19, Lanise Padilla, 16, and 15-year-old Cornelius McCullum[28]. "This is the path they chose, and now they're facing adult consequences for the decisions they made," said Albuquerque Police Officer Fred Duran[29].

A small group of teens, without any "territory" or hand in the drug trade, without real colors or hierarchy, and yet look what they managed to accomplish. We must remember that criminal enterprise is a growth industry, even for small start-ups like crews.

Prison Gangs

Prison gangs can be considered the graduate school for street gang members. There exists a misconception that, once a criminal is incarcerated, they are on the path to rehabilitation. The fact is, many of these gangs control the actual living fabric of prison life and in most cases, maintain control of their streets from behind bars.

Born in prisons but extending out into the streets, once prison gangs get their claws into a street gang member, their education in criminality and its obligations takes on an advanced status. This is one reason why advocates say juveniles should not be jailed with adult offenders, as juveniles are easy prey for prison gangs. Once they are recruited, the rehabilitation process is daunting and the child's future and even their life is at risk.

Much of the onus to join a prison gang is motivated by the need for self-preservation in the shark tank of opposing factions that is the correctional system. Juveniles, if prosecuted and incarcerated as adults, are especially easy prey for predators the minute they cross the prison threshold, and gaining the protection of an established gang, usually one based along racial and ethnic lines, is perceived to be the only choice for survival.

Once a juvenile who has joined a prison gang is released, their street cred has grown significantly because they are considered to have "paid their dues" by doing the time and coming out alive, more emboldened to expand their criminal activity with the backing and support of the gang.

Dominant prison gangs in the U.S. that have expanded their grip from the prisons to the streets include:

1. Aryan Brotherhood

2. Barrio Azteca

3. Mexican Mafia (La Eme)

4. Nuestra Familia

5. Tango Blast

The Barrio Aztecas in particular provide some insight into ways gang culture is made attractive to juveniles, even outside benefits of protection and supposed wealth. The BAs are among the most violent gangs in the United States, but which few outside the southwest have ever heard of. Founded in 1986 by Mexican and Mexican-American inmates from El Paso's Segundo Barrio in the Coffield Unit of the Texas Department of Criminal Justice prison (rising in opposition to the existing criminal organizations of the Texas Mexican Mafia and Texas Syndicate), the BAs quickly rose to criminal prominence in the region, eventually serving as the street enforcement arm for the Juarez Cartel.

The BAs distinguish themselves by proudly conjuring images of pre-Columbian Aztec culture, in particular their reputation for being fierce and feared warriors. The iconic image of the warrior Popocatepetl holding the lifeless body of his love, princess Iztaccihuatl, is prominently used. And, as it happens, the typical Aztec became a warrior at about seventeen years old—just around the time many prospective BAs join the organization.

Outlaw Motorcycle Gangs

Outlaw motorcycle gangs are typically not an attractive option for teens, nor are OMGs known for going out of their way to recruit teenage members. That's not to say teens don't feel any allure from the roar of motorcycles and the intimidation these gangs exude when they enter a community; it's just much less common than some of other gang types we've discussed, with the average age of OMG members being somewhere in their thirties and forties. In fact, most OMGs have a minimum age requirement of eighteen years old, which may be due to the age required to obtain a motorcycle license, the drinking age of twenty-one, or having the ability to purchase and maintain a bike.

Dominant OMGs in the U.S. include:

1. Bandidos

2. Cossacks

3. Hells' Angels

4. Mongrals

5. Pagans

6. Vagos

GANG LIFE

Before actual initiation into a street, prison, or OMG, there is typically a feeling-out period where the gang evaluates the recruit's potential contributions, whether as an earner through drug sales, extortion, enforcer, prostitution, or gun sales. Ultimately, the decision made by the gang's hierarchy will be based on their ability to trust the prospect to be a contributing and functioning member of the gang—one who is loyal to the death, will put the gang first above everything, will never divulge gang policies or secrets, and who will represent the gang at all times, regardless of the risks.

The actual initiation process could involve a variety of criminal tasks, including robbery/burglary, rape, or even a murder to prove their loyalty and toughness. It may also involve a "jump in." Depending on the gang, this period can last for varying lengths of time, and involves other gang members circling around the recruit and brutally pummeling him with punches and kicks. MS 13 requires their prospects to endure a thirteen-second beating by multiple members, which is typically followed by hugs and hand slaps signifying their acceptance. The cuts and bruises sustained from this sort of hazing can be a telltale sign for educators and parents that the teen has entered a gang. In the case of girls, some gangs offer the choice of either a "jump in" or being "sexed in," where they have sex with a predetermined number of gang members. While most gangs still sexually objectify their female members, there is a growing trend to "use them more functionally," since they don't always garner the attention of law enforcement and can use their female acumen to better infiltrate other gangs.

Unsurprisingly, it's hard to escape a "jump in" unscathed. In the wake of the turmoil created by MS-13 on Long Island, the New York Post interviewed a former gang member, "Speedy," who described his experience; how, at sixteen he endured his jump in by gritting his teeth so he didn't scream out in pain while they beat him relentlessly for thirteen seconds: "Three gang members kicked and punched me all over my body—my arms, my back, my stomach, my hands, even my groin. Nothing was off-limits to them. Moments later, I was in so much pain I could barely stand up. But eventually I grew to enjoy beating others."[30]

Once in a gang, there is typically no safe way to retire; "blood in, blood out" is the expression, owing to the suspicion that a member leaving the gang could be dangerous to the gang, and deadly to the person leaving. Leaving a gang often requires the member to move in order to get away from the gang's influence. But it can be done. After five years with his gang, Speedy had had enough and wanted out. He told the other gang members of his intention, but they refused his request. "They said I had too much information," Speedy relates. "I left anyway, and they shot up my house. Luckily no one was around. That's when I went to a different place. I had to leave Central Islip [Long Island] to get my life back"[31].

"Speedy's" case is not unique. Thousands before him have seen the light of a life outside the self-destructiveness of gangs. By no means is escape the only option; there have been countless others who have returned to their hoods, defying the gangs to become leaders of young children aiming to offer them an alternative perspective on life and what the future holds for them. This is still a potentially dangerous proposition for the reformed gang member but the impact their presence has on the youth in their community is more valuable than any social worker coming in from the suburbs.

A fundamental strategy for leaving a gang is to have an escape plan, both literally and figuratively. It's very hard to escape the grasp of the gang without assistance from trustworthy individuals who can be relied upon not to betray the person leaving the gang. The next step is determining where to go, and what short and long-term resources are available in terms of housing, food, security, and social/substance abuse rehabilitation. Former gang members can also benefit from receiving counseling to address underlying post-traumatic stress disorder, a common issue as life in a gang can be as traumatic as combat. Many gang members have seen the death of a fellow gang or family member or had to murder an opponent. Their life is consumed in a state of hypervigilance waiting for oppositional retaliation. Ignoring the aftereffects of a life of traumatic exposure puts the individual at risk of using drugs and/or alcohol to "deaden" the pain and to calm themselves down.

GANG SUPPRESSION

The best way to suppress a gang is to get ahead of their criminal activities, which means being proactive. Unfortunately, issues with staffing make it difficult for most police departments to be aggressively proactive. Only rarely do most communities notice or appreciate the fact that they have a gang problem until the bodies start piling up; most residents won't even notice the human trafficking or drug dealing unless they or a family member is directly involved. I've spoken to law enforcement all over the country, and while the majority say that gangs fester in their schools, the administration does not want to do anything about it.

Ignoring cancer cells like these in their early stages is what allows them to metastasize throughout a community and region. Suppression must be a holistic approach between law enforcement, schools, social welfare, religious and community organizations, and the families themselves. If gang members are dealt with sternly at the outset of their criminal behavior, the future outcome may be different.

WARNING SIGNS OF GANG PRESENCE

The first step towards recognizing and defending against gangs in your community is to learn the warning signs of their presence. Remember: where there is one, there will be more. Parents and teachers must be cognizant of these warning signs so immediate intervention can be implemented.

Signs for Parents and Educators

While it likely will not make me any friends among the younger generations, the truth is that a child does not have the expectation of privacy in their house. A good parent will look at social media accounts, observe any behavioral changes, any new groups of dubious friends, different clothes or hair styles, listen to the music their child likes, and question them if there are any concerns. Whatever involves your child *is* your business. Schools are a different story, but educators can still identify warning signs and immediately contact the parents if they suspect anything. If it seems like the parents are ambivalent or possibly part of the problem, then the police should be called. Time is of the essence in these matters, and the deeper a teen gets into gang life the greater the consequences and more difficult it is to get out.

A teen entering gang life will exhibit the majority of these behavioral traits:

- Withdrawing from family or becoming defiant and argumentative beyond typical teenager behavior.
- Truancy, declining school performance, and behavior issues resulting in detentions or suspensions.
- Staying out late without reason and not saying or else lying about who they are with. (Teens out after midnight are

either up to no good or run the risk of being victimized by someone who is. Parents need to impose and enforce reasonable curfews.)

- Displaying an unusual desire for privacy or secrecy; does not want parents to enter their bedroom or look at their social media accounts.
- Exhibiting signs of drug and/or alcohol use.
- Consistently and defiantly breaking family rules such as curfew and chores.
- Trouble with police or school officials.
- Obsession with gangster-influenced music, videos, movies or websites.
- Has unexplained cash or purchases of jewelry, clothes, electronics, and even vehicles.
- Students coming to school beaten up. While this may be a case of traditional school bullying, injuries may also be a result of a student's "jump in". They may attempt to conceal the cause of their wounds and bruises.
- Being found in possession of or concealing a weapon on their person or in their room.
- Admits to membership in a gang. Some gang members, especially young or newly minted members, will proudly strut their colors as a sign of belonging and their newly obtained power and respect.
- Calls from people the parents don't know and who speak in ways that might indicate they are lying or attempting to conceal their identity, talk in one-word statements, or just sound like a thug. Caring, involved parents typically have pretty good intuition, which shouldn't be underestimated.
- Empty spray paint cans around the house or even inexplicable spray paint on the teen's hands, possible indications of tagging or vandalism.

SIGNS FOR COMMUNITY MEMBERS

The first step in suppressing gang activity in your community is to recognize you have a gang presence, even before it turns into a gang problem. Do not fall into the trap of shrugging off criminal activity as actions of "wannabe" gangsters. A gang problem in a community, even a small one, does not require the validation of a major gang franchise to pose a clear and present danger to the community. Even five local teens calling themselves a gang can still create a public safety issue.

Recognizing a gang presence requires a proper understanding of the dynamics of gangs, from member demographics to the types of crimes typically committed, the criminal enterprises they are most frequently involved with, their area of operation, rivals and allies, recruitment methods, locations, targets, etc. Having this information will enhance targeted enforcement strategies by law enforcement and the municipality, who may be better able to step in to improve living conditions or boost social and recreational programs.

In addition to these signs, the general community needs to be aware of common indicators of gang activity in their area, to serve as watchdogs against possible gang insertion.

These include some or all of the following:

- Graffiti in school bathrooms, desks, books, and community buildings. This may be the work of a banal tagging crew with no criminal intent other than vandalism, but for gangs, such practices are intended as an early marker of their presence or to stake their claim to an area, as well as creating intimidation among rivals and the community.
- Increased incidence of vandalism in a community. For gangs, especially if it is a new one, this is a beginning step towards more

drastic criminal behavior. They may be testing the waters to see how much they can get away with.

- Burglaries of homes and businesses. These often fuel drug habits of members as well as provide a source of revenue and (potentially) weapons.
- Inexplicable rise in violent crimes. This usually is the result of turf or drug trade conflicts.
- Visible signs of young people congregating, flashing hand signs and wearing similar colors. This can be seen in school hallways classrooms, shopping areas, movie theaters, and other public places.

Intelligence

On that note, developing intelligence that can be used for targeted enforcement operations is key. This includes interagency cooperation as well as corrections, and intra-agency intelligence should also not be neglected. Corrections and police should have a close line of communication. As an example of the need for this, gangs such as MS-13 are now getting away from wearing visible tattoos to avoid police scrutiny. A gang member may be arrested without the police officer even realizing they are a gang member because it is only when the suspect arrives at the jail and a strip search is conducted that tattoos obscured on the inside of lips, trunk, or other areas not seen by the field officer emerge. The jail will likely record this gang affiliation, but this does little good to public safety if the information is not conveyed to the arresting agency.

In addition, trained school security and local police resource officers need to work hand-in-glove when sharing information with patrol officers and vice versa. Gang activity typically emerges in schools where recruiting is easy and productive, and emerging trends can be seen in the closed environment before they hit the streets.

Community Policing

Community policing, which must be sensitive and trained in the language and culture of the community they are patrolling, is essential. There are countless well-intentioned young police officers who come from predominately white communities, only to be stationed in minority communities with socio-economic dynamics they are ignorant of or completely blind to. For instance, I've often had to stress to officers that not all "Hispanics" are the same, as unwary officers can think that everyone who speaks Spanish is the same. Puerto Ricans, Salvadorans, Mexicans and Dominicans, for instance, are *not* all the same; they have distinct differences in dialect, food and cultural norms. Officers in these positions should be encouraged to demonstrate an interest in learning the culture by reaching out to the community, as this will reap immeasurable rewards, not the least of which is gaining the community's trust. Police have the ability to use discretion in minor offenses, and people in these communities have long memories of good and bad police behavior. This discretion can help nurture information on criminal behavior sources.

Stop, Question, and Frisk is a controversial police tactic, but when implemented properly and constitutionally, can send a powerful message: that we know who you are, and we are watching. Unfortunately, many agencies abuse this tactic beyond its intended use—to look for concealed weapons—and have alienated many in the communities they were supposed to protect.

Finally, monitor legitimate businesses suspected of being used as a front for illegal activity. This is often seen with OMGs where members may have a motorcycle repair or supply business or a bar. (Other businesses can be convenience stores, laundries, tattoo parlors, etc.)

Quality of Life and Public Image

Communities should address quality of `life crimes committed by gangs through enforcement of civil ordinances on things like party houses, loud car speakers and tinted windows on vehicles. These initial steps can be effectively used to lead investigators to suspects with warrant violations, weapons possession, and drug trafficking. Don't neglect the little things. Small bait can lead to big fish catches.

Similarly, cities must cover over gang graffiti as quickly as it appears. This mitigates the gang's claim to your community. One strategy that can work is to have arrested gang members do the job in conjunction with a counseling program, either as part of their sentence or probation.

School Policies

Implementing zero tolerance policies in schools like strictly enforced dress codes for students and anyone picking a student up from the school can do a lot to slow the spread of gang activity in schools. Besides, the last thing a school needs is to have two opposing gang member parents showing up simultaneously to pick up their child.

School officials should look to train their custodial staffs to be aware of gang graffiti around the school and, before cleaning it, be sure to photograph it and identify the location. This should then pass on to the school resource or security officer, who should then pass the information on to local law enforcement. This chain of intelligence is valuable in proactive policing and school policies.

On top of this, institute truancy sweeps. This is huge, yet controversial, but there is an indisputable link between truancy and crime[32].

The link between truancy and crime clearly emerged during Chicago's crime wave. Reporters for the Chicago Tribune scoured court, prison, and school truancy records and found that between 1999–2007, some three thousand students a year in grades K-8 were officially listed as dropouts, a number which spiked to 6,625 in 2008[33]. The cases appear endless, but include two fourteen-year-old dropouts, one of whom was arrested for aggravated assault and theft, who dropped out in the seventh grade. The other sold heroin[34]. The authors found that the natural trajectory for these teens is becoming "foot soldiers" for gangs[35].

There are myriad strategies to explore for implementation of truancy sweeps, but in order for them to be effective they *must* include the full commitment of law enforcement, schools, parents, and the municipality.

Cooperation with Immigrant Communities

Law enforcement must gain the confidence of immigrant communities, especially in cases like MS-13. There is justifiable fear among the illegal immigrant community in the U.S., who find themselves wedged between the rock of gang intimidation and the hard place of fear of deportation. This is a constant public relations struggle for law enforcement since they need the cooperation of the victimized community to apprehend the gang members who are terrorizing them.

This is another facet of effective community policing: reaching out to a community to let them know law enforcement is there for them. Most of these individuals struggled and paid exorbitant fees to come to the U.S. and are working hard to support their families; their hard work should not be compromised by gang activity.

Another option to explore are two visas—the "S" and "U" visas—which are available, albeit in limited numbers, to immigrants who are either victims or who are cooperating with law enforcement.

The **S Visa** is for individuals living in the U.S. illegally but who are willing to assist law enforcement, and is a substantial benefit for witnesses and informants who might not otherwise be able legally to enter or remain in the United States and who provide critical, reliable information necessary to the successful investigation or prosecution of a criminal organization[36]. The major obstacle there, both for the immigrant and law enforcement, is that Congress only authorizes two hundred of these visas annually[37].

The other option is the **U Visa,** which is for victims of crimes, the result of legislation intended to "strengthen the ability of law enforcement agencies to investigate and prosecute cases of domestic violence, sexual assault, trafficking of aliens and other crimes, while also protecting victims of crimes who have suffered substantial mental or physical abuse due to the crime and are willing to help law enforcement authorities in the investigation or prosecution of the criminal activity."[38] The mandated granting cap for the U Visa is much more generous than the S Visa, with 10,000 visas granted to principal petitioners each year. There is also no cap for family members deriving status from the principal applicant, such as spouses, children, or other eligible family members[39].

Accountability and Oversight

Parents must be held accountable for the actions of their children. Many parents of troubled teens are hardworking people just trying to survive, but the majority do not supervise their children, or else have domestic conditions that fuel criminal behavior. Yet very rarely are parents held accountable. Charges of child neglect should be considered, especially if there is precedent for criminal behavior in the house being conducted by parents or other family members.

Likewise, sponsors of unaccompanied alien children who do not comply with their federally mandated obligations must be held to answer for any and all negligence on their part. Like deficient parents, UAC sponsors should face similar prosecution for child abandonment. Since more than eighty percent are in the country illegally and already facing deportation proceedings, there needs to be more aggressive enforcement.

Legal Recourse

While this is more in regards to state and federal treatment of gang activity than community proactivity, aggressive use of state and federal laws like RICO (Racketeer Influenced and Corrupt Organizations)/VICAR (Violent Crimes in Aid of Racketeering Activity) for large gangs and federal weapons charges may provide for longer terms of incarceration with guilty verdicts. These federal statutes have been effectively used to prosecute MS-13, Barrio Azteca, and some of the bigger gangs, and prosecutors in states that have weak or absent gang laws should explore cooperating with federal prosecutors to file federal weapons charges against any gang members from large and small organizations.

Similarly, the use of gang enhancement policies, where additional sentencing time is imposed at conviction due to the suspect's affiliation with a gang and if the crime was committed at the behest or furtherance of the gang, can serve as a potential deterrent.

Gang suppression should include a combination of these suggestions, but first and foremost, they must be legal and constitutional. Being well-intentioned but violating an individual's civil rights only results in cases getting dismissed, compromising strategic effectiveness and credibility.

Ideally, strategies should be data driven. Numbers help with funding and program efficacy. Sometimes numbers and funding are not available, especially in early program stages where supporting metrics are not yet available. In order to address a need or crisis, sometimes you have to go with your gut and common sense to solve a problem. It's better to do something, fail, and then modify it, than to do nothing at all. The effort will at least demonstrate that the problem has been identified.

More prevention strategies will be discussed further in a later chapter, but suffice it to say that extraordinary measures need to be implemented by families, schools, community organizations, and social services to involve children in productive activities and raise them in caring and nurturing environments.

CONCLUSION

Gangs have been a part of the American social fabric for nearly two hundred years. Their creation stemmed from immigrant and minority groups seeking protection from the dominant population in a region, only to resort to criminal activity, mostly within their own community. Some of these gangs have evolved into sophisticated criminal organizations that transcend borders, having a significant impact on crime.

To combat this deep-set and entrenched criminal subculture, early identification, prevention, and suppression strategies must be holistic in nature, incorporating resources from law enforcement, schools, the municipality, social services, and parents. Procrastination and ignorance of addressing a gang problem in a community will only allow it to spread.

CHAPTER 4

LOST SOULS: ADDRESSING SCHOOL SHOOTINGS

"Be tolerant of those who are lost on their path. Ignorance, conceit, anger, jealousy and greed stem from a lost soul."
—NATIVE AMERICAN CODE OF ETHICS:
ELDER WISDOM

ON APRIL 20, 1999, the sanctity of American schools was changed forever. On that cool and breezy Tuesday morning, two students arrived at the school shortly after 11 AM, curiously wearing full length trench coats. Eighteen-year-old Eric Harris and seventeen-year-old Dylan Klebold methodically proceeded through Columbine High School in Littleton, Colorado, an affluent and quiet Denver suburb, and began systematically shooting an arsenal of weaponry at students and staff. When the shooting ended, there were twelve students and one teacher dead, and twenty-one wounded. As law enforcement closed in to try and quell the carnage, the two each fired a single bullet into their heads, ending their own lives in the same methodical way they had carried out the well-planned massacre[1].

The reasons behind this volcanic eruption of violence have been debated by pundits and arm chair psychiatrists. Three months after the massacre, while evidence and memories were still fresh, the FBI and a team of credible experts examined the root causes behind Harris and Klebold's attack. What they found was a history of mental illness fueled by a narcissistic superiority complex, with the root cause being to satisfy a desire to commit a mass murder of epic proportions[2].

There were numerous warning signs both at home and at school that should have sparked concern but were ignored: Harris and Klebold had expressed admiration for the likes of Adolph Hitler and Charles Manson in school assignments; Peter Langman, Ph.D. writes in a blog entry for Psychology Today.com examining the psyche of Harris and Klebold[3] that the mass casualty incident was not merely a by-product of bullying, since both perpetrators had bullied other students themselves; it is indisputable that Harris was taking the anti-depressant Luvox and had anger issues; the duo had even videoed themselves displaying weapons and explosive devices they intended to use at school that fateful day. No one connected the dots, and the result was the school and the nation at large paid the deadly price of ignorance.

Little did the friends, who referred to themselves as the "Trench-coat Mafia", realize that their horrific attack would ring in the new millennium with a crescendo of debate over gun laws, treatment for the mentally ill, school security, and perhaps most disturbingly, validation for a new generation of similarly struggling teens who would express their anger at society or individuals in the same manner. School gun violence, though rare, was nothing new; but Columbine was obviously something different, and not just because of the double-digit casualty numbers—it awakened a nation to how unheard cries for help and ignored warning signs could play out in similarly tragic fashion.

It is worth noting, however, that Columbine was *not* the first mass shooting at a U.S. school. That ignominious honor goes to twenty-three-year-old Charles Whitman's spree, which saw thirty-three killed and twenty-three wounded at the University of Texas on August 1, 1966. It was later learned that the blonde crew cut engineering student had a brain tumor that may have contributed to his irrational act. Prior to his suicide on the campus bell tower that he used as a sniper perch, he wrote a suicide note where he requested an autopsy to see if he had any disorders, even making reference to his being a "victim of many unusual and irrational thoughts."[4]

Though Columbine was not the first, it was by no means the last, either. A month later to the day, fifteen-year-old Thomas Solomon, Jr. of Heritage High School in Conyers, Georgia, wounded six students in a school shooting intended by Solomon to be an homage to the Columbine shooters, and an attempt to replicate that catastrophe. The sophomore was described as a pleasant student who attended church, and was even a Boy Scout[5]. He had recently experienced a break-up with a girlfriend, but most telling was his depression diagnosis and a prescription for Ritalin[6]. At the end of the tragedy, Solomon threatened to kill himself by placing a .357 magnum in his mouth, but was talked off the ledge and taken in. He was ultimately found guilty of murder in the shooting but was considered mentally ill. After serving sixteen years in prison, he was paroled to his mother's recognizance in July 2016.

It wouldn't be until 2005 that another mass school shooting would rock a community, this time on the remote Red Lake Indian Reservation in Minnesota when sixteen-year-old Jeffrey Weise killed his grandfather and his companion before driving to his high school and killing five students, a teacher and security guard, wounding seven others before taking his own life. He allegedly faced incidents of bullying and a disrupted homelife but it was his bout with depression, which included two suicide attempts and the prescribing of Prozac, that should be considered foremost in the discussion.

The tragedies started to mount at this point, occurring periodically. In 2007, Seung-Hui Cho, 23, killed thirty-three and wounded twenty-three at Virginia Tech. Ten days before Christmas 2012, twenty-year-old Adam Lanza killed his mother in their home, and four teachers, the principal, school psychologist and twenty first graders at Sandy Hook Elementary School in Newton, Connecticut. This tragedy is still impossible to reconcile. Parents should be buying their seven and eight-year-olds toys for the holidays, not burying them. Both shooters would commit suicide.

Fast forward to 2018, where two major school shootings occurred and reignited the call for legislation and better preventive measures provided to students. Valentine's Day is a traditional occasion for expressions of love and affection, but this wasn't the case on February 14, 2018, when Nikolas Cruz entered Marjory Stoneman Douglas High School in Parkland, Florida. The previously expelled student systematically killed seventeen and wounded fourteen. Investigators found social media posts they said were "disturbing" and Florida Governor Rick Scott called the incident "pure evil"[7]. School officials said Cruz was frequently disciplined for "deviant behavior"[8].

Cruz faced a life of adversity. When he was three years old, he was diagnosed with developmental disabilities and three years later witnessed the death of his father to a heart attack. School records described him as lost, lonely and violent, and in eighth grade, he was assigned to a school for students with emotional problems. Among his more compelling diagnoses were depression, attention deficit hyperactivity disorder, emotional behavioral disability, autism, obsessive-compulsive disorder and anger issues[9].

The most recent school shooting occurred as I wrote this chapter. In Santa Fe, Texas on May 18, 2018, Dimitrios Pagourtzis, 17, killed ten and wounded ten at Santa Fe High School. A student identified Pagourtzis as "really quiet, and he wore like a trench coat almost every day"[10]. In typically balmy southeast Texas, the sight of a teen wearing a trench coat over a T-shirt that read "Born to Kill" should have sparked concern—but it didn't. Not until the shotgun blasts echoed through the halls. Pagourtzis's motive is said to be based in his being spurned by a female classmate who rebuked his advances[11].

The complexity of these incidents is underscored by the ambiguity of a headline covering the tragedy in the New York Times: "In Texas school shooting, 10 dead, 10 hurt and many unsurprised"[12]. Yet based on the reporting, many in the school *were* surprised. Pagourtzis was described by one teacher as "quiet, but he wasn't quiet in a creepy way." "He was an introvert, not an extrovert"[13]. Even Governor Greg Abbott was given no information that would have raised concern: "We have what are often categorized as red-flag warnings, and here, the red-flag warnings were either nonexistent or very imperceptible."[14]

From a statistical standpoint, mass shootings in schools are rare, but this makes them no less devastating to students and their families. The thought of a parent kissing their child goodbye in the morning and hoping they can make it through the day alive is one that should never become normal. For the despondent student considering suicide, which most shooters either contemplate or carry out, perhaps the thought of not dying in anonymity, of "going out in a blaze of glory" is a preferential end to their inner struggles.

This is a daunting yet profound concern that has emerged in the wake of Columbine. In the past, at-risk children would internalize their angst, whether caused by "bullying" or mental illness. At some point, something changed, and the thought of annihilating dozens of classmates and teachers, most of whom had nothing to do with the troubled student's angst, became seen as a legitimate option for these disturbed individuals. It wasn't until Columbine and Klebold and Harris's dastardly act that a mass shooting became a form of validation, a way to express one's self-worth. Intentionally or not, Klebold and Harris appear to have opened a Pandora's box for a new generation of troubled teens to express their anger in similar fashions.

The rise of mass school shootings can be linked to a cultural domino effect of institutional failures that have left at-risk youths wallowing in their pain to the point that committing acts of inexplicable violence against people who never contributed to their percolating anger becomes perceived as a viable option.

Among these failures can be included:

The Elimination of the Personal Approach to Teaching

The effects of standardized testing and practices such as "No Child Left Behind" and the Core Curriculum program have essentially eliminated the personal approach to teaching. "We teach to the test," is now the common retort among teachers. (I experienced this first-hand during a brief stint as a middle school language arts teacher on the Navajo Reservation.) This results in an inadvertent set of blinders being put on as teachers become overwhelmed with the real and perceived expectations of their profession. Student interaction and observation become blurred and there is a reluctance to "label" students who demonstrate problematic behavior.

The Disintegration of the American Household

Regardless of whether it is a dual or single-parent home, modern financial demands now often preclude intensive supervision of children, who are left with their thoughts to fester into potentially destructive outcomes. A lack of parental attention can also contribute to child anxiety and depression. Parents, consumed with their own lives and concerns, often leave their children by the wayside, even when confronted with the failings of their child. This is not endemic just of lower income families, either: I have observed this just as fre-quently in affluent families where the parents' social life supersedes the raising and nurturing of their children.

The Failure of the Mental Health System

There are limited resources available for teens, and what resources do exist are costly. The de-emphasis on institutionalization has kept many vulnerable people on the streets despite their need for long-term care, which includes condition-specific counseling and supervision of medication prescription and administration. Unfortunately, parents are once again complicit in this struggle. They oftentimes do not want to acknowledge their child has something wrong and instead deprive them of the care they need, both for their own well-being as well as the safety of others.

Misuse of Psychiatric Medications on Children

Researchers estimate that one in eight children under eighteen years old have a depressive episode[15]. By the mid-1980s the go-to treatment was selective serotonin reuptake inhibitors (SSRIs) for depression and Ritalin for attention deficit disorder-hyper-activity disorder. Between 1987–1996 the prescription of anti-depressants to children under eighteen increased tenfold[16]. The prime purveyors of these prescriptions were not psychiatrists but pediatricians (twenty percent of all prescriptions) and family physicians (more than forty percent[17]).

Relying solely on medications to alleviate their young patient's angst, there was rarely any accompanying in-depth questioning as to what may be causing the depression or the concurrent prescribing of counseling. As for Ritalin, there is still an ongoing debate as to what hyper-activity *is*, much less what ought to be done for its treatment. In a 2016 article in the Washington Post, fully a third of the six million children in the U.S. were reported to have been diagnosed with ADHD[18] and that American children may be overprescribed medications such as Ritalin, whose side effects can include, among a plethora of others, nervousness, agitation, and psychosis[19]. As far back as 2004, the Food and Drug Administration found the medications increased the risk of suicide and issued a public warning, although the National Institute of Mental Health found that the benefits of these medications outweighed the risks to children[20].

A March 2018 report by the Citizens Commission on Human Rights International found the following medications had the highest rates of violence as compared to other drugs[21]:

Fluoxetine (Prozac): 10.9 times

Paroxetine (Paxil): 10.3 times

Fluvoxamine (Luvox): 8.4 times

Venlafaxine (E exor): 8.3 times

Desvenlafaxine (Pristiq): 7.9 times

Sertraline (Zoloft): 6.7 times

This brings us back to the mass school shooters. As mentioned previously, some of the worst mass school shooters in American history were prescribed an anti-depressant. There is also an anecdotal link between the explosion of prescriptions and shootings. Around the same time that the prescription of anti-depressants was increasing dramatically, the Columbine massacre occurred. Admittedly, the number of mass shootings compared to the eight million or so children on anti-depressants or medications for ADHD is miniscule. What can't be ignored is that many of the school shooters *were* on these medications. If we are to mitigate these tragedies, there needs to be a more concerted effort to address juvenile depression. Medication should only be part of the solution and not the end-all panacea. Perhaps the FDA needs to re-examine who should be permitted to prescribe these medications, along with issuing specific guidelines that include some kind of psycho- or behavioral therapy component. A pediatrician or family physician would never think of performing open heart surgery; so, why should they consider prescribing psychiatric medications despite lacking the training required to do so?

Determining what a child is depressed about should be the first step in any treatment plan; you can't fix what you don't know is broken. Is the child depressed because of family strife? Grades? The current obsession over and concurrent pressure exerted on students to be successful on standardized tests? Self or parental imposed unrealistic expectations in academics or an extra-curricular activity? A struggle with sexual orientation? A romantic breakup? Bullying?

This sort of questioning frequently does not occur in an initial doctor's visit, and pediatricians and family physicians are not extensively trained in how to get to the root problem. As a result, they prescribe medications based solely on symptoms. This is akin to prescribing a pain killer to treat the headaches of an undiagnosed brain tumor. This is a grave disservice to the child and possibly public safety. Not to mention, parents need to be included in the strategy as well, certainly beyond just picking up a prescription at the pharmacy and ensuring the child is taking the medication as prescribed. Various cognitive therapies should be discussed with trained professionals then carried out at home, teaching the child skills to identify and address the causes of their depression. Medication can be a valuable tool as long as it is taken as prescribed and monitored by a physician.

GUNS

Having discussed the elements that make up the shooter, we must segue into the realm of the actual instruments used in these tragedies—guns.

Discussing the role of guns in mass shootings and the related issue of gun control is a volatile topic in today's discourse. On the one hand you have the chicken and the egg issue of, "Guns don't kill people; people kill people." The recent uptick in mass shootings in America has sparked a viscerally reactive attitude towards gun policy, one that requires taking a step back and examining what actually went wrong in these tragedies, how guns came into play, and what we can best do to ensure public safety effectively.

It is hard to debate or be critical of the millions of legal gun owners in the U.S. who have never killed someone, as compared to a few dozen shooters who wreak havoc in our schools. We can't vilify everyone for the actions of a few, nor should we look at penalizing those who aren't responsible.

The issue with teen mass shooters comes down to a potential result of what can go wrong when weapons aren't treated with the respect they deserve, and are placed in the hands of the mentally unstable (regardless of whether said instability is acute or chronic). Very rarely in the political arena is responsibility put at the feet of the parents, for example, who knew their child had a mental illness and still kept accessible guns in their home. This access to weapons by school shooters does not follow the paradigm of gun safety, one advocated by those on both sides of the issue, including organizations like the NRA, which has come under increasing fire as the conversation over gun control continues to escalate.

In fact, in many of the cases we've mentioned the parents were inadvertent accomplices; or, in the case of Adam Lanza's mother, a victim. Adam Lanza is a prime example of what happens when the perfect storm of mental illness and access to weapons occurs. Prior to his nonchalantly walking into Sandy Hook Elementary School, the twenty-year-old had a history of mental illness that was left mostly untreated, despite his mother being an educator. According to published reports, Lanza had a history of anxiety, obsessive-compulsive disorder and undiagnosed anorexia, among other issues that his mother refused to appropriately address[22]. "It was his untreated mental illness that was a predisposing factor," says Dr. Harold Schwartz, chief psychiatrist at Hartford Hospital's Institute of Living[23].

Most compelling was an observation made in a report released by the Connecticut Office of the Child Advocate examining Lanza's history and lead-up to the massacre. The report said Lanza displayed "severe and deteriorating internalized mental health problems" and was still allowed to "retain access to numerous firearms and high-capacity magazines" in his home[24]. The report went on to say that, "His parents, and certainly his mother, seemed unaware of any potential detrimental impact of providing unfettered access to firearms to their son"[25]. Nancy Lanza would pay for her ignorance by being the first victim on that fateful day, which ended with her son taking his own life.

More recently, the parents of murdered Santa Fe High School student Chris Stone have filed a lawsuit against Antonios Pagourtzis and Rose Marie Kosmetatos, parents of shooter Dimitrios Pagourtzis, alleging they failed to properly secure their weapons (a .38 caliber handgun and a sawed off shotgun), permitted their son to have access to their weapons and ammunition, failed to obtain mental health counseling and services for their son, failed to properly warn the public of Dimitrios' "dangerous propensities," and negligently entrusted their weapons to their son[26]. The lawsuit dramatically proclaims, "Had the murderer not had available to him the weapons for his carnage, his hidden black rage might well have continued to simmer within, but, the life's blood of his teacher and peers, including DECEDENT CHRISTOPHER JAKE STONE, would not have been so horribly, callously and needlessly spilled"[27].

These are high-profile cases where parents violated the tenets of proper gun security in homes with children with emotional disorders. This combination of denial of there being any problem with a child and the accessibility to guns is what contributes to mass shooting incidents. After the gunfire has subsided and a shooting has been properly and thoroughly investigated, those parents who are found not to have secured their weapons, whether they know their child has a problem or not, should be held accountable. In the case of Texas, where the Pagourtzis' live, there is an added caveat in state law that stipulates gun owners should, "take steps that a reasonable person would take to prevent the access to a readily dischargeable firearm by a child, including but not limited to placing a firearm in a locked container or temporarily rendering the firearm inoperable by a trigger lock or other means."

Which isn't to say that the parents are always to blame in this fashion. More recently, Nikolas Cruz, the shooter at Marjory Stoneman Douglas High School in Florida, legally purchased the AR-15 assault rifle he used to kill seventeen on Valentine's Day 2018. There were apparently no difficulties in his obtaining an automatic weapon, despite his dubious background that agents would not have even needed to access before determining whether he could legally buy the weapon.

There is a glaring loophole in passing the background check required before purchasing a gun, dealing with whether the would-be buyer has a mental illness. A mental illness only disqualifies an individual from purchasing a weapon when the individual is adjudicated mentally defective or has been committed to a mental institution. The majority of people diagnosed as depressed and put on medication, for example, do not appear as red flags in the standard searches.

So, what can be done? Should physicians be compelled to submit the names of all patients put on anti-depressants to a federal data base as it relates to gun purchases? Obviously, this would create great outrage, as well as be deemed a violation of the Health Insurance Portability and Accountability Act, citing a breach of patient privacy. Yet this is the major fault in the system: there is virtually no way to identify these at-risk individuals when they purchase a weapon. In Cruz's case, he was diagnosed with depression and had stopped receiving treatment over a year before the shooting[28].

Parents, educators, school administrators, and law enforcement need to work together to mitigate the occurrence of these tragedies, all of which can be prevented with proper communication, policy and foresight.

SCHOOL SHOOTING PREVENTION

Effectively preventing a mass school shooting requires looking at the threat in its totality, in the same way that a municipality prepares for a terrorist attack. In the wake of the new era of awareness following Columbine, schools, police and emergency medical services have drastically revised and improved their response procedures. Students now periodically practice lockdown procedures to ensure they are prepared in the event of an emergency.

Yet, based on my experience with schools as a teacher, a parent, and a law enforcement instructor, students and staff still need much more training to be truly prepared for an active shooter incident. Passively going through the motions of a lockdown scenario during a midday drill does not realistically address the issue, especially since the paradigm needed during an active shooter event—"Run-Hide-Fight"—doesn't even address lockdown. As a result, when the shooting begins the fog of confusion is often magnified by students left out in the open.

Training realistically, as law enforcement does, will better prepare students and staff for an actual incident. For example, incorporating exercises where police use air soft guns and wound simulations at least prepares students for the stress involved in such a crisis. Experts also contend that students should also be taught what options to exercise if they are required to "fight," as well as what might be effective options to employ. Facing an armed suspect when your life depends on it is a situation few of us can imagine, but having some foundation of self-defense can be lifesaving.

Students should also be oriented on what law enforcement does and doesn't do when responding to an active shooter. For example: police engaging an active shooter do not prioritize immediate care for the wounded. While it may be traumatic to observe police walking over the wounded, their primary role in these incidents is to find and neutralize the suspect.

However, schools are reluctant to insert this sense of realism into their drills out of fear the students will be traumatized. A teacher in Halfway, Oregon sued her school district after alleging she suffered post-traumatic stress disorder after going through a surprise mock active shooter drill in her middle school in 2013[29]. In the mock drill, fifty-six-year-old teacher Linda McLean said a masked man ran into her classroom, put a pistol to her face and screamed, "You're dead!" Another teacher reportedly wet herself when a "shooter" went into her classroom and fired blanks.

Officials conducting the drill said a majority of teachers in the school would have died in a real attack, citing their unpreparedness. This was a compelling evaluation, and one that should not be taken lightly. Our society is rarely prepared for such incidents because we find the training for them to be distasteful and upsetting. Yet security experts agree that, given the new era of school shooters and terrorists, we need to emulate the mindsets of countries like Israel, where every citizen is trained and prepared for the worst-case scenario, so that when it occurs there is an appropriate response.

Cooper's Color Code System

Devised by the late U.S. Marine Lt. Col. Jeff Cooper, the color code system for situational awareness is a defense tactic used by both law enforcement and the military, and one which every student should be made aware of. Take a moment from your busy day and look around at the behavior of the people around you. They might be talking or texting on their cell phones, or walking with their heads down, or talking to a companion. What they *aren't* doing is keeping their head on a swivel, remaining cognizant of their surroundings. A student showing up in a trench coat to a school in southeast Texas on a warm and humid spring day should be a red flag; a student walking into a school with a backpack and a glassy forward stare, not acknowledging anyone may be a predicator to a shooting.

Cooper's Code is a method of delineating certain behaviors as being part of high or low situational awareness and is ordered along a grade of colors. These four stages are:

White Stage. The individual is essentially oblivious to what is going on around them. They are texting or talking on their phone or just lost in their thoughts. These are prime mugging targets, especially during the holidays. In your typical school setting where no one ever thinks a shooting will occur, white stage individuals are a common sight. This is the stage that students need to be most instructed about to enhance their chances of not being victimized.

Yellow Stage. Your head is on a swivel, but you are able to go about your daily activities because there are no threats. You are geared up "just in case". This is the stage we need to teach our children to be. Just telling them about "Stranger Danger" or "See Something, Say Something" is only part of the equation, particularly if they cannot recognize potential threats. In this stage you should be looking at where you are and what are your options to run or hide.

For students and school staff, discussions should be held as to what the options are for every classroom used. Can you escape out of a window? What if you are on the second floor? What will you use to lock the classroom door? What can you use to fend off the attacker if necessary?

Items such as fire extinguishers have been advocated as viable options to at least temporarily incapacitate a suspect, giving you time to escape the threat. Having training in self-defense tactics to manipulate a weapon from a shooter may also give you time to disable the threat but not necessarily take their life.

These are all things you don't want to have to think about *during* a shooting.

Orange Stage. This stage is reached when a potential threat is recognized—noticing the student coming into school on a warm day wearing a trench coat. What is your plan? Where are you going to run to? Where are you going to hide? What form of communication will you have to summon police? Are you prepared to fight and if so, with what? Having the answers to these questions already in hand is the benefit of first passing through the Yellow Stage.

Red Stage. In this stage, there is a recognized and active threat on your life. You will need to know what to do if you no longer can run or hide. If you have to fight, what are your Yellow Stage plans? You need to know what to do and do it fast!

TACTICS FOR PREVENTING SCHOOL SHOOTINGS

School shootings should be looked at with the same concern as any terrorist attack, in terms of what should and can be done to prevent or mitigate the loss of life. There are a series of considerations that should be part of any school shooter prevention plan:

Threat Assessment

By undergoing a comprehensive threat assessment, you earmark what the potential for a shooting could be at your school. As recent events indicate, every school is a potential target and the threat that it can happen at your school should be taken seriously.

In your threat assessment, you will want to determine any structural, personnel, or policy weaknesses at your school. This is best determined by an impartial source not affiliated with the school district who will come in with a fresh, unbiased set of eyes. Ideally, the threat assessment should be performed by local law enforcement, not only to assess the school's vulnerability but to also assess and pre-plan how officers will access different parts of the school in the case of an active shooter. This can save valuable time in response and evacuation of students.

Items to look at in a threat assessment include options for access to the school that a shooter can take, and how students can escape the school (egress options). The Santa Fe School District in New Mexico, for example, has taken the proactive measure of being the first in the country to install a revolutionary anti-intruder technology in their schools[30]. Their simple lock system is quickly activated by the flick of a finger. "The objective here is, even under severe duress, just by touching the device with your finger or with your toe it automatically goes into the floorplate and it's locked down," said inventor Ed Johnson. "And once it's locked down there's absolutely no getting through that door without ripping out the doorframe." Regardless of what device a school chooses, there should be primary locks on all classroom doors that can easily be activated by students or staff, as well as a device that can block the door from opening should the lock malfunction.

Intelligence

Schools will never admit to gathering intelligence on students for fear of violating civil rights, but there are ways to recognize or follow up on warning signs observed by teachers, students, and parents that pertain to potential at-risk students who may perpetrate a school shooting. The most basic way this can be done is for teachers to read student assignments. Student writings can reveal a lot of pain and a desire to harm others as a form of personal validation. For example, the Columbine students were found to have written some disturbing essays in response to assignments they were given.

Another method for gathering intelligence is social media. Reviewing social media sites should be done by both parents and teachers. These sites are open sources of information that carry with them no expectation of privacy. Moreover, students have posted some extremely disturbing messages on social media that serve as precursors to violence.

Even graffiti found in and around the school can be seen as sending provocative messages and should at least be considered as potential harbingers for future violence.

Of course, all observations and information should be evaluated for validity. Rumors are an unfortunate part of school culture, and therefore any information gathered should be rigorously scrutinized and verified before any action is taken. This may initially be in the form of bringing the concerns to the parents of the student, though ultimately child welfare and law enforcement may need to be included.

TRAINING IN RUN-HIDE-FIGHT

The "RUN-HIDE-FIGHT" paradigm has long been the accepted paradigm in situations involving active school shooters. There has recently been close scrutiny as to whether this is actually the best paradigm to follow, but most agree that the solution, if any, will be to incorporate training for participants such that flexibility can be built into the existing system.

RUN

The RUN element of the active shooter paradigm makes sense as part of an effort to escape the shooting itself. However, students and school staff need to be trained as to when and where to run, as well as when it is appropriate to put the students in a classroom lockdown. They must also be instructed to leave all their items behind and keep their hands raised when confronted by police. I have observed many schools conduct lockdown exercises but saw few that instruct students on where to run, how far, and how to communicate their whereabouts with authorities—all difficult decisions that students may not be able to make on the spur of a chaotic moment. In a 2015 article for PoliceOne.com[31], the author identifies a lack of "mental conditioning" typical in the U.S. when it comes to facing a shooting situation, and notes the increased risk that potential victims will freeze, referred to as "panic induced paralysis", when confronted with a shooter. He also expresses concern about the linear thinking that typically comes with a systematic paradigm like RUN-HIDE-FIGHT, which leaves people thinking that the FIGHT component should be the last resort, when in fact it may be the immediate best option.

On the topic of lockdown, while this may be an option it is not always the best choice, especially if there are inadequate methods of securing doors in a crisis event. Additionally, most of the weapons used by recent shooters can easily blow out a school door lock if the shooter so desired. If lockdown is to be the school's response protocol, there needs to be a diligent effort to install primary and secondary classroom locking mechanisms. Something as simple as a wooden door jamb placed on the inside of the door can delay a shooter if they blow out the door lock, as can stacking desks against the door (if time permits).

HIDE

HIDE, the second aspect of the paradigm, is a good option if you have the opportunity. But students caught in the middle of a cafeteria or in a hallway will have limited options for hiding. Students need to be taught that in order for them to receive the benefits of hiding, they will need to be sure their entire body is kept out of view. Hiding under a desk or table with your feet hanging out does no good.

One major component of effective hiding is stealth. The problem with this is that shootings are inherently traumatic. There is a lot of screaming, crying, and hyperventilating, all of which can give away your location. Students need to be trained on how to calm themselves to remain silent as the shooter moves through the building. Making noise while hiding defeats the purpose. One other suggestion, one which should be done anyway for unrelated reasons, is to have students silence their cell phones, not turn them off. Cell phones can provide valuable intelligence to police who are preparing to enter the school in terms of suspected number of shooters, victims, and your location.

FIGHT

The FIGHT stage should be done immediately if the opportunity presents. You may not have time to RUN or HIDE if the shooter is standing in front of you. When police are not yet in the building, it may come down to you to stop the carnage.

However, if you *are* going to fight, you need to be one hundred percent committed. Hesitation will not end well. The goal is to distract, hinder, or subdue the shooter to allow others to escape. It *is* possible; ordinary people have performed extraordinary tasks in the face of danger. This was aptly demonstrated by Indiana middle school teacher Jason Seaman in May 2018, when he immediately confronted a student holding two handguns and shooting at students in a science class at Noblesville West Middle School by throwing a basketball and charging at the shooter while yelling for students to take cover. Although Seaman sustained multiple gunshot wounds, he survived, and is credited with saving the lives of his students. "Our science teacher immediately ran at him, swatted a gun out of his hand

and tackled him to the ground," student Ethan Stonebraker said. "If it weren't for him, more of us would have been injured for sure."[32]

Methods of how to fight back against a shooter are constantly emerging but what needs to be stressed is that whatever device or method is used, it needs to be done quickly and violently. Suggestions range from staplers to scissors to school books for use as improvised weapons.

Arguably one of the most creative strategies was employed at a Pennsylvania school district. Blue Mountain School District in Schuylkill County now stores five-gallon buckets of river rocks in every classroom in the district to be used in case of an active shooter. ""If an armed intruder attempts to gain entrance to any of our classrooms, they will face a classroom full of students armed with rocks, and they will be stoned," said school superintendent David Helsel[33]. Helsel paints an impactful picture of twenty-five students and a teacher throwing rocks at a shooter and how effective that could be. I have to admit, it is a low-cost solution to a significant problem—as long as the threatened parties are prepared to do it.

ARMING TEACHERS

THERE HAS BEEN discussion regarding an increased armed police/security presence in schools, a conversation which has extended to arming teachers. As might be expected, the debate has quickly become heated; the thought of a teacher being armed, on the surface, appears to some to be repulsive. Kenneth S. Trump, President of National School Safety and Security Services, expressed his concerns by saying, "School districts considering arming teachers and school staff with guns would take on significant responsibility and potential liabilities that I firmly believe are beyond the expertise, knowledge-base, experience, and professional capabilities of most school boards and administrators."[34] He goes on to say, "Educators enter a profession to teach and serve in a supportive, nurturing role with children. To ask them to abruptly kick into the mindset to kill one of those same students in a second's notice is not realistic"[35].

By the same token, Trump's concerns do very little to protect students, as Jason Seaman aptly demonstrated. Teachers are inherently responsible for the safety of their students. The inability of a school to protect its students by not having adequate resources to confront an active shooter should not be considered an unfortunate necessity. And the issues Trump raises are not without solutions: concealed carry license holders, for example, go through a rigorous curriculum that includes liability, teaches use of force, and instructs as to the potential ramifications of using a weapon in self-defense.

Of course, before this discussion can even be put into action lawmakers would have to be supportive of such an initiative and pass legislation to protect an individually armed teacher and the school district in cases of the justified use of a firearm to protect students from an active shooter. The Castle Doctrine, for example, is commonly used to defend homeowners who practice lethal force in cases where their life or that of their family members is threatened by an intruder. A similar type of legislation can be considered to protect school personnel. The other benefit to an armed teacher in this sort of crisis scenario is that they know the school and may have an easier time locating the shooter before police arrive.

In the absence of arming teachers, schools are more seriously evaluating positioning armed security or police in their hallways. Many schools already have precedent for this, in the form of school resource officers (SROs)—typically armed officers from the local police department or sheriff's office who are regularly posted in schools (typically junior and senior high schools). Their role in mitigating an active shooter can be invaluable if properly trained and motivated.

Unfortunately, this wasn't the case with the SRO at Marjory Stoneman Douglas High School. During the school shooting perpetrated Nikolas Cruz, Deputy Scot Peterson came under extreme criticism for failing to follow active shooter protocol and aggressively seek out and neutralize the shooter. Granted, from what we have seen in other incidents, these sorts of lukewarm responses are extremely rare; police on-site will throw themselves into the line of fire to protect students. Officers *can* be highly successful in saving lives, as was the case in Dixon, IL. In May 2018, SRO Mark Dallas immediately and effectively responded to an attack on Dixon High School by nineteen-year-old Matthew Milby, who began shooting near a graduation rehearsal. Dallas' quick response prevented any students from being injured; he immediately gave chase on foot to subdue Milby, who opened fire on the officer, but Dallas was able to return fire and wound the shooter.

Schools and communities need to look more seriously at school security. Arming teachers, despite the controversy surrounding it, may not even be the best option, as SROs are much better trained and will have only one task in these incidents: to neutralize the threat.

OTHER PREVENTION PROGRAMS

In recent years there have been other programs professed to be more appropriate for an active shooter response. They are ALICE and Move! Escape or Attack.

ALICE

ALICE stands for Alert, Lockdown, Inform, Counter, Evacuate. In the **Alert** stage, the threat is recognized, and there is need for immediate action to be taken. **Lockdown** is just as the name implies: classes should be locked and barricaded to prevent the intruder from entering. **Inform** sees administrators communicating with staff to provide situational awareness and instructions, in addition to conveying real-time information to law enforcement. **Counter** is any effort to distract, disrupt, or subdue the shooter. **Evacuate** is the safe and strategic exit from the building under fire.[36] Similar to RUN-HIDE-FIGHT, ALICE should be implemented in the context of a fluid situation, and should not be adhered to rigidly; the context of the moment must dictate necessary action. For instance, teachers may have to **Counter** before being able to put the school on lockdown.

Move! Escape or Attack

Move! Escape or Attack is another option, one which seems to have more inherent flexibility by virtue of not being as structured as the other two paradigms. This means less chance for confusion if a step is skipped because of the situation. In Move! Escape or Attack, the key is to, when in doubt, MOVE away from or EVADE the shooter. Keep your head on a swivel and know where you are going to move or escape to; you don't want to run to a locked door or dead end.

When in doubt, remember the "X" rule. In law enforcement and the military, the "X" is the point of contact. When the shooting starts, students and staff need to be taught to immediately flee from the "X".

Escape is a continuation of Move! You are looking to increase the distance between you and the shooter, or at least obscure yourself from his field of vision. If he can't see you, he can't shoot you. **Attack** is when all else fails, you don't have the time to escape, or you have the opportunity to subdue the threat sooner rather than later.

Whatever system your school deems more viable, it is imperative that it is practiced regularly and as realistically as possible. Sugar coating these drills does a disservice to the potential victims. I would argue that it is better to deal with the anxiety of a drill than the carnage of an active shooter. Situational flexibility must also be instilled in the training. How students and staff adapt to the chaotic fluidity of these situations must be considered.

EMERGENCY FIRST AID

An unfortunate reality of any active school shooting is the horrific wounds rendered by the array of weapons typically used in these attacks. These can be as benign-looking as a small hole to the gruesome wounds created by a high-velocity rifle. The injury may have just an entrance wound, meaning the bullet has tumbled around the inside of the body causing extensive damage, or it can have an entrance and exit wound.

Minutes count in a survival situation but, as has been stated, professional care is delayed until the shooter is neutralized. Police will walk over the wounded and not render care until their primary goal is accomplished. This is why tactical first aid classes for schools are so important: wounds that occur in active shooter incidents transcend typical first aid techniques. A gaping wound to the thigh that cut the femoral artery will not respond to direct pressure, with the victim dying in as little as three minutes, just about the time police arrive to confront the shooter.

If schools want to explore functional methods of keeping students and staff alive until professional care arrives, tactical first aid training should be provided as an adjunct to basic first aid.

This training should include the following:

- Proper application of a tourniquet and chest seal. If there is a steady flow or spurting blood coming from a wound the immediate application of a tourniquet is necessary to save life.

- Proper response for a sucking chest wound. This injury occurs when a bullet or knife penetrates the chest and air builds up in the chest cavity, placing pressure on the heart and adjoining lung and resulting in death if not cared for. There will be a hissing or sucking sound coming from the hole with each breath as well as frothy pinkish blood around the wound.
- Treatment of shock. Learn to recognize the signs/symptoms of shock, including decreased alertness, weak or rapid pulse, cool or clammy skin, fatigue, chest pain, etc. Makeshift care for shock involves wrapping the victim in a blanket. Be sure the blanket is also placed between them and the ground, since a lot of body heat can be lost this way.

All other wounds can be treated with basic first aid and CPR skills as necessary. All school staff and students should be trained in first aid and CPR. Remember: in the case of an active shooter, everyone is a potential caregiver.

CONCLUSION

The title of this chapter, Lost Souls, describes exactly what these young people are: those who have fallen through the social, medical, and educational cracks, and are truly lost souls. They decide to pick up a weapon, walk into a school and shoot innocent children. Schools should be a sanctuary for learning and child development. Parents need to feel confident that when they kiss their child goodbye in the morning, they will be sitting at the dinner table with them that night.

This is no longer the case. Now, every parent has to wonder whether their child will be safe at school. And the reality is that these attacks are likely to continue, as there has been very little change since the start of this new era of school violence to suggest otherwise. Our culture of poorly supervised prescription of anti-depressants, limited or misused mental health resources, fear of labeling a student a potential attacker, validation of bad behavior secondary to a lack of student accountability…the list goes on.

There *are* things that can be done. It begins with the recognition that, while we want to maintain a pleasant school atmosphere, one that isn't intimidating, the fact is that as soft targets schools need to revisit whether they are more concerned with appearances or security. Regular drills that are as realistic as agreeably possible, which include law enforcement must be conducted at least once a semester. Self-defense and first aid training should be part of a comprehensive active shooter plan.

Security in schools must definitely be tightened through policy changes, structural modifications, and armed security. The debate over whether teachers should be armed can be alleviated by school districts and communities providing funding to have on-site school resource officers who are specifically trained to deal with active shooter scenarios and have the resources on hand to neutralize these threats.

This conclusion may appear pessimistic, but above all we must be pragmatic. These incidents are occurring, and at a disturbingly increased rate. If we are to ensure the safety of our schools and children, we must recognize the situation as one of crisis and be prepared to aggressively confront it. Our children deserve no less.

CHAPTER 5

SOCIAL MEDIA: NOTHING "SOCIAL" ABOUT IT

"Social media policies will never be able to cure stupid."
—NICHOLE KELLY

"**SUGAR AND SPICE** and everything nice." That was once the way little girls were described, as the transition from childhood to adolescence was heralded by a changeover from ribbons and bows in their hair to dabbling with makeup and jewelry. As the father of three daughters, I lived this emotionally daunting experience firsthand. But for two young Florida girls in 2013, ages twelve and fourteen, their transition into jewelry was the silver of handcuffs after being implicated in the cyber bullying of a classmate—a classmate who felt jumping to her death was her only option to escape a torrent of vicious and targeted social media posts.

Twelve-year-old Rebecca Sedwick of Lakeland, Florida was a typical American pre-teen. Pictures of her show a bubbly smile and a sparkle in her eyes; a ribbon on her shirt reveals a future of hope and promise. That is, until an older girl began dating a boy Rebecca had previously dated. The older girl began a Facebook campaign of ridicule and torment against Rebecca, either out of spite or in revenge for the sorts of comments teens typically make in times of emotional upheaval. "They would tell her she's ugly, stupid, nobody liked her, go kill herself," said Rebecca's mother, Tricia Norman to the media after her daughter's death[1]. Other, similarly abusive messages from the older girl coaxed Rebecca to "drink bleach and die," all while enjoying her time spent with the new boyfriend.

By the time of Rebecca's suicide, officials say the number of girls involved in the escalating digital campaign of terror had grown to as many as fifteen individuals. Following Rebecca's death, which resulted from jumping from a cement mixing tower, one of the girls maliciously posted on Facebook, "Yes ik [I know] I bullied REBECCA nd she killed her self but IDGAF [I don't give a (expletive)]"[2]. As might be expected in today's society, where a lack of accountability for one's children's actions is common, the parents of the older girl not only refused to cooperate with police, but said, "My daughter's a good girl, and I'm 100% sure that whatever they're saying about my daughter is not true"[3]. In the end, the older girl was charged with aggravated stalking, a third-degree felony in Florida.

Rebecca's tragedy is not unique. Campaigns of social media bullying are rampant in today's social media obsessed society, and is an issue which requires a much more aggressive investigation into whether this abuse serves as a contributing factor to teen violence—whether self-inflicted or as a catalyst to cause harm to others. Suicide is the second leading cause of death among teens and, increasingly, fingers are being pointed at social media as a cause. Researchers have found, based on a survey given to approximately two thousand middle school students, that victims of cyberbullying were almost twice as likely to attempt suicide than those who were not bullied[4].

SOCIAL MEDIA

The proliferation of social media use has increased exponentially and has become permanently ingrained in world culture—for better or for worse. Social media was instrumental in spreading the word in the Arab Spring and other social uprisings, as the platforms allow for word to get out fast to millions of people with virtually no cost or effort.

According to Statista[5], social media is used by more than two billion people around the world and is expected to grow to nearly three billion by 2020. The report said that eighty percent of the U.S. population has a social media account, with ninety percent of that number between the ages of 18-29. In another report provided by Statista, the preferred social media sites for teens were Snapchat, Facebook, Twitter, and Instagram, with those in the 16-24 demographic spending an average of two hundred minutes per day on a mobile device[6].

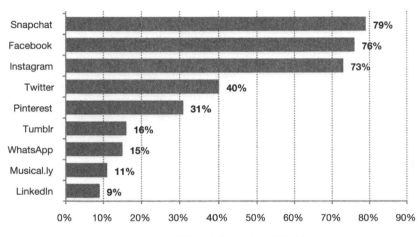

PERCENTAGE OF RESPONDENTS

Yet the term "social media" is somewhat oxymoronic; the purposes these platforms are used for go far beyond simple social interaction. We have seen political discourse, personal shaming, institutional complaints, and other anti-social behavior run amok, all with the benefit of anonymity. Our society has been conditioned to find every personal idiom worthy of being announced to millions of viewers on Facebook, Twitter, Flickr, etc.; at the same time, these platforms are also being abused by a growing number of teens as a portal to bully those they dislike anonymously—not just in their group of immediate friends or classmates, but the entire world.

Facebook's stated mission is "to give people the power to share and make the world more open and connected." On its site, Facebook explains that it believes increased connection between people through their site will lead to better understanding between disparate groups. As an ideal, this is laudable. But in practicality; laughable. The level of social erosion we have seen since the advent of social media is alarming and is a problem that must be understood and addressed. We have seen how hyper-connectivity can devolve into a catalyst for acts of self-inflicted harm and violence against others.

Abuses of social media such as cyber bullying and "revenge porn" reveal a darker underlying nature in some users of social media. It is a fact that anonymity emboldens people, and with this confidence has come a host of individuals wielding social media like a weapon, striking out with impunity. This makes it extremely tempting for disconnected abuse of others, while for the victim the constant abuse becomes inescapable.

CYBER BULLYING

The data we have supports the extensive use and abuse of social media among young people. And while it has yet to be designated a public health crisis, its implications can't be ignored.

CYBERBULLYING BY THE NUMBERS

- Eighty-seven percent of today's youth have witnessed cyberbullying.
- Close to thirty-four percent of students acknowledge that they have experienced cyberbullying.

- Fifteen percent of students admit to cyberbullying others.
- Twenty-four percent of children report that they would not know what to do if they were harassed online.
- Thirty-nine percent of children do not enable privacy settings on social media.
- One out of three kids feel they are more accepted on social media networks than in real life.

Commonly Reported Types of Cyberbullying

- Nineteen percent of cyberbullying entails the spreading of rumors.
- Nearly thirteen percent of victimized children experience hurtful comments.
- Seventy-two percent of children report they are cyber-bullied because of their looks.
- Twenty-six percent of victims are chosen due to their race or religion.
- Twenty-two percent of harassed children feel that their sexuality was the cause of their bullying.
- The National Autistic Society reports forty percent of children with autism and sixty percent of children with Asperger's Syndrome report experiencing bullying, both on and offline.

Cyberbullying by Gender

- Girls (forty-one percent) are more likely to experience cyberbullying at some point in their life compared to boys (twenty-eight percent).
- Girls who cyberbully tend to post mean online comments.

- Girls tend to favor social media outlets like Snapchat or Instagram while boys often interact over gaming consoles.
- Male cyberbullies often post hurtful photos or videos.

The Effects of Cyberbullying

- More than seven out of ten children report that bullying negatively impacted their social lives.
- Eighty-three percent of victims felt that the bullying hurt their self-esteem.
- Thirty percent of victims have turned to self-harming behaviors, which has increased by six percent from 2013.
- Thirty percent of children who have been bullied have suicidal thoughts, a five percent rise from 2013 statistics.
- Ten percent of children have attempted to take their own lives due to bullying.
- Seven percent of victims have bullied others as a result of their torment.

Data provided by TeenSafe[7]

Based on this data, we can see how all the developmental pitfalls of adolescence—insecurity, self-esteem issues, worries about appearance, and behavioral traits—can all be exploited by those who find reason to digitally abuse others.

The adolescent trait of not fully comprehending or appreciating the consequence of their actions also comes into play. Offenders typically give as their excuse for cyberbullying that they were only joking, or they didn't think the victim would take the posts so seriously or didn't think it was going to result in someone harming themselves. Yet as we have seen repeatedly, cyberbullying *does* result in self-inflicted violence.

SUICIDE

Suicide is among the most egregious forms of teen violence. Not to say that any form of wanton violence is justified, but when it comes to a young person self-inflicting harm because of an acute or chronic deluge of attacks against their self-esteem, it moves beyond the pale. The cumulative impact of cyberbullying on already-vulnerable teens is devastating and contributes to the equally devastating American suicide statistics. Worse, most of these children feel they are forced to suffer in silence. Rarely do they show their parents the vulgar texts or embarrassing photos someone else posted to shame them.

Compounding this issue is the wealth of information freely available on the internet. Information on suicide cases that may be replicated by a vulnerable teen; methods for committing suicide, providing a person with a number of options; an anonymous communication method to form suicide pacts with other vulnerable teens; exposure to those who encourage suicide as a means of dealing with distress; suicidal ideation and predilection; and perhaps most disturbing, the ability to self-post one's own suicide.

The research into this social dilemma is just now emerging. Variables still have to be weighed for each incident as to whether and to what extent the bullying was cyber or verbal, in public or in private, what the teen's pre-suicide state of mind was, and how cyber bullying contributed to the death. Regardless of specifics, however, the use of social media as a weapon by teens against other teens should be seen as detrimental and shouldn't be downplayed.

Over the past twenty years there has been a concerted effort to identify and prevent the root causes of bullying. Most states have some semblance of legislation to address this, as do schools who constantly attempt to nip incidents before they escalate onto the playground and classrooms. StopBullying.gov describes bullying as any unwanted, aggressive behavior that involves a real or perceived power imbalance[8]. This aggressive behavior may be verbal, physical, and/or written, as in the form of social media posts. There's very little distinction with cyberbullying, which is increasingly more prevalent because of its convenience, reach, social impact, and of course, anonymity.

ACCORDING TO STOPBULLYING.GOV, the following are signs that bullying is taking place.[9]

Verbal bullying is saying or writing mean things. Verbal bullying includes:

- Teasing
- Name-calling
- Inappropriate sexual comments
- Taunting
- Threatening to cause harm

Social bullying, sometimes referred to as relational bullying, involves hurting someone's reputation or relationships. Social bullying includes:

- Leaving someone out on purpose
- Telling other children not to be friends with someone
- Spreading rumors about someone
- Embarrassing someone in public

Physical bullying involves hurting a person's body or possessions. Physical bullying includes:

- Hitting/kicking/pinching
- Spitting
- Tripping/pushing
- Taking or breaking someone's things
- Making mean or rude hand gestures

To emphasize, bullying is *not* synonymous with suicide. Unfortunately, it has been a part of growing up for millions of children for generations. But where past generations would push past the pain as they get older and put the incident into perspective, this seems to be inexplicably happening less and less as time goes on. Perhaps there is a boomerang effect resulting from the increased efforts to raise awareness. In other words, the increased focus on awareness may actually be inflating the impact we see on children. If this is the case, it would seem more effective to empower children to stand firm and be resilient in the face of adversity, rather than teaching them to self-identify as a victim.

That being said, parents don't necessarily have to put their child on suicide watch if they feel they are being victimized by bullying; however, neither should this issue be ignored if the potential for self-harm exists. Children who exhibit risk factors should be monitored closely and counseled immediately. The Center for Disease Control and Prevention says that, "In reality, most students have a combination of risk and protective factors for bullying behavior and suicide related behavior"[10]. The federal agency goes on to say that the factors that can increase suicidal vulnerability include emotional distress, exposure to violence, family conflict, relationship problems, lack of connectedness to school/sense of supportive school environment, alcohol and drug use, physical disabilities/learning differences, lack of access to resources/support.[11]

Compounding these risk factors is the feeling, on the part of the victimized teen, that they are alone in their battle against persecution; that nobody understands or would know how to help them. Adult intervention is often perceived by the victim as being "babied," which contributes to more abuse. There might even be a sense of shame or embarrassment over what may have precipitated the bullying, such as a perceived/real physical anomaly or a photographed incident of lapsed judgement. These factors all need to be included in the examination of this problem and assessed in their totality if a successful outcome is to be reached.

In December 2016, Brandy Vela, a senior at Texas City High School, who had been the victim of a sophisticated campaign of cyberbullying shot herself in front of her father, who was pleading for her to stop. The reasons behind what amounted to a campaign of terror against Vela were not disclosed, but the level of sophistication and effort involved reveals a level of malice and derangement rarely seen in cyber bullying. Vela had received abusive text messages for months from an untraceable smartphone application; a fake Facebook page was created using her name to further harass and shame her. Her mother, Jacqueline, said Brandy struggled with her weight. "They would make dating profiles of her, and they would put her number and they would put her picture [on the sites] and lie about her age and say she is giving herself up for sex for free, to call her." Brandy would change her phone number, only to have her tormentors locate it again somehow[12].

By November 29, 2016, Brandy was at the end of her rope despite her parents' support and the filing of reports with school and law enforcement officials. As the holiday season was in full swing in the Houston suburb, Brandy sent an email to family members that she was at home and was about to kill herself. When her father Raul arrived, he found his distraught daughter against a wall in her bedroom crying, with a gun to her chest. As her father tried to discourage Brandy from taking such a drastic measure, a shot rang out. "We tried to persuade her to put the gun down, but she was determined, she said she'd come too far to turn back. It was very unfortunate that I had to see that. It's hard when your daughter tells you to turn around. You feel helpless"[13]. To add insult to injury, Raul Vela reported that the cyber harassment continued even after Brandy's death.

Two suspects were arrested in connection with the tragedy, one of whom was an ex-boyfriend of Brandy's. In March 2017, police arrested Andres Arturo Villagomez, 21, and his then-girlfriend Karinthya Sanchez Romero, 22. A Galveston, Texas Grand Jury charged

Romero with stalking and online impersonation, felonies punishable by two to ten years in prison in Texas. Villagomez was charged with misdemeanor unlawful disclosure or promotion of intimate visual material but could only be sentenced to up to a year in jail[14]. This is little consolation for the Vela family, who will remember Brandy's text message for the rest of their lives: "I love you so much just remember that please and I'm so sorry for everything."

It's heartbreaking to think that Brandy and thousands of other teens are choosing to end their lives as a response to senseless and callous bullying. Among the many questions raised by episodes like this one, chief among them is what can cause the sort of emptiness in another person that they feel compelled to destroy another person's life in such a vicious fashion. There is a plethora of triggers that can lead a child down the path to becoming a bully, oftentimes unbeknownst or even ignored by the parents. Among these are a conflict with a sibling or adult family member; inherent low self-worth that is projected onto their victim; a desire to demonstrate physical dominance; a lack of empathy for others; a propensity to dominate others; and transferring pain they may be experiencing at home against a weaker individual.

BULLYING UNDER THE LAW

As if being bullied by a peer isn't bad enough, the introduction of adults into the fray has demonstrated another brick out of place in the social foundation of America. In 2008, Lori Drew, 49, was convicted in federal court on misdemeanor charges related to the relentless cyberbullying which led thirteen-year-old Meghan Meier to hang herself. Drew fabricated a social media page of a sixteen-year-old boy, whom Meghan communicated with until the "boy" sent her a message saying, "The world would be a better place without you." Meghan hung herself with a belt in her bedroom[15]. The motive behind the deadly scheme, which included Drew's thirteen-year-old daughter, was not revealed.

In a case that didn't have any statutes to back up a stiffer charge, the fact that Drew conducted her activities with her daughter should have at least elicited a charge of contributing to the delinquency of a minor or other similar charge. Yet law makers are still barely catching up with technology in their efforts to address the prevalence of cyberbullying. Every state has some semblance of an anti-bullying law or policy; the sanctions range from merely symbolic in some areas; all states except New Mexico, Wyoming, Nebraska, Minnesota, New Hampshire, and Maine, have legal sanctions if convicted.[16]

In some areas, the school districts themselves are responsible for setting a policy. Yet suspensions and expulsions, a school's primary disciplinary recourse, are no consolation for the long-term pain this behavior creates for the victim and their family. Many of the charges should fall under harassment or harassment communications. In Arizona, for instance, the individual would face harassment under subsection A, a class 1 misdemeanor (harassment under subsection B is a class 5 felony).

Where the laws fall short, the parents of bullied victims who ultimately committed suicide are taking to the civil courts to hold parents accountable for the actions of their children. In 2017, the parents of twelve-year-old Mallory Grossman, a New Jersey middle school student who killed herself due to bullying, sued their school district for allegedly doing nothing to intervene in the cyberbullying campaign against their daughter, which included messages urging her to kill herself, despite repeated attempts to bring it to their attention. Similar to the arrogance displayed by the parents of the girls who tormented Rebecca Sedwick, the night before Mallory died a parent coldly told Mallory's mother that, "It was just a big joke, and that [she] really shouldn't worry about it"[17].

ANTI-BULLYING STRATEGIES

One strategy being employed by victims and parents is to turn the tables on the bully by legally and publicly shaming them through an actual lawsuit. While the possibility of reaping any rewards from suing a minor is remote, the opportunity to publicly and legally pronounce their bad deeds is compelling. Suits have already been filed in a few incidents. In 2011, Houston attorney Jason Medley issued a cease and desist notice to three female students at Riverwood Middle School and their parents in Harris County Civil Court after they uploaded a video they compiled attacking his daughter. Medley also ordered the parents to donate $5,000 to the non-profit organization Safe and Responsible Internet Use[18]. He went on to say that if the terms were not met, he would file a lawsuit directly against the girls for defamation of character.

"I think this father is trying to be a parent that the other girls do not apparently have," said Nancy Willard, founder and executive director of the Center for Safe and Responsible Internet Use. "Think of the lesson he is teaching his own daughter: You do not have to put up with someone hurting you. You can calmly and strongly say 'stop,' and I have your back."

As Willard alludes to, this is an extremely novel approach: suing teenage girls who essentially have no viable assets or source of income to support a claim for punitive damages. However, in close knit communities the light that Medley shed on the accused girls and their families could be overwhelming.

In 2012, a female teenager sued two classmates for derogatory comments they posted on Facebook. As a result of the posts, Alex Boston, 14, withdrew from social contact and became depressed. Her parents reported the harassment to local law enforcement who could provide little comfort and support after they told the family to notify Facebook and request that the inflammatory account be shut down. Receiving no relief, the Bostons sued the girls responsible for the cyberbullying, as well as their parents for providing the internet service and digital equipment, stating their actions were, "intentional and malicious and were done for the purpose of causing Plaintiff to suffer humiliation, mental anguish, embarrassment and emotional and physical distress."

When children and parents receive no relief from their anguish from either school or law enforcement officials, the only other legal recourse is to seek a remedy in civil court. Battling a bully is best done by standing up to them, turning to a comfortable support mechanism, or ignoring them and finding an activity that provides a build-up of self-esteem. The problem is that these options may not fit in a vulnerable teen's narrative, opening the door to self-harm (in the form of suicide) or public retribution, lashing out violently at the world that ignored or perpetuated their pain.

RETRIBUTION

The 1999 Columbine High School shooting served as a wake-up call for America. All was not well in the hallowed halls of our schools; disgruntled students could now take up arms, walk into their school and begin shooting.

It also sounded an alarm as to the new ways teens were coping with bullying. No longer would they suffer in silence or commit a lonely act of suicide. What emerged in the wake of the shooting is that Eric Harris and Dylan Klebold *were* bullied and they *did* contemplate suicide, but ultimately decided to express their anguish in a violent fashion first.

Antonios Pagourtzis says his son Dimitrios was bullied, causing him to lash out at classmates at Santa Fe High School in May 2018:

"Somebody probably came and hurt him, and since he was a solid boy, I don't know what could have happened. I can't say what happened. All I can say is what I suspect as a father." A student would corroborate Pagourtzis's presumptions about bullying. What wasn't understood at the time was that it wasn't just students doing it: "I know he's picked on by coaches and other students. He didn't really talk to anyone, "My friends from the football team told me that coaches said he smelled, like, right in front of his face. And other kids would look at him and laugh at him…nothing, like, physical but they still emotionally bullied him"[19].

CRIMINAL ACTIVITY AND SOCIAL MEDIA

The use of social media by gang members, euphemistically referred to as Cyberbanging, is surprisingly pervasive despite the risk they run of being noticed. Utilized as a means to recruit, intimidate, and boast of their exploits, it's more often seen among young gang members who feel they have something to prove to older gang members, or who have a sense of invincibility, however naïve, that they won't be noticed by law enforcement.

A survey of five hundred current or former gang members conducted by University of Colorado Sociology professor David Pyrooz found that gang members use social media as much if not more than the general public[20]. Pyrooz found that gang members are not reluctant to display their counter-culture behavior; rather, social media gives them a platform to validate a distorted sense of self. "Gang members mostly go online to post photos and videos that perpetuate their tough image," says Pyrooz[21].

However, gang-related social media activity is not benign and transcends mere boasting. There has been a growing trend towards the use of emojis as a sort of coded message system. Gangs will taunt each other by posting "drill rap" videos, which typically include the displaying of guns, gang hand signs and expressions of disrespect or promises of violence against their rivals. "We have seen situations where someone will commit a shooting or a homicide, and they'll immediately write something on social media," said Matt Anderson, a Richmond, California gang detective. "'Man down,' 'scoreboard;' those are the kinds of phrases they'll use, and it gives us a lot of clues about what just happened"[22].

Warring gangs in Detroit go so far as to post photos of rival gang members they have marked for death[23]. These "Hit List" posts are a trend that demonstrates the precipitous downward spiral of this medium. Officials in Detroit reported that of the ten gang members marked for death in one such flurry of posts, seven were shot, four fatally, and three escaped attack are likely laying low because of the veracity of the posts.

As prolific as gang members' use of social media is, it is one of the first places law enforcement goes to investigate crimes, effectively intervening both to prevent violent incidents and to use as a tool to effect arrests. Like a trail of bread crumbs, diligent law enforcement officials can effectively trail a digital footprint. If they have a suspect(s) in mind, it provides an easy starting point to constantly follow posts and their respective expressed attitudes. Police can actually "stake out" a social media platform and wait for the suspect to post incriminating information that can be used to prevent or solve a crime.

Just as gang members use social media to boast of their exploits, law enforcement has increasingly adapted to the ever-evolving technology and have used social media to reach out to victimized communities seeking help or to provide tips anonymously. Most law enforcement agencies around the country have some form of social media to provide tips and even photographic or video witnessing. In some instances photos and videos are uploaded in real time, identifying suspects, locations, vehicles, weapons, or victims. These are very effective in solving crimes and provide a valuable option for those in the community who "don't want to get involved" but do want to provide police with crime-related information. One of the most effective advances has been the implementation of agency Crimestopper sites, where witnesses can anonymously email law enforcement tips to aid in solving crimes.

EXPLOITATION

It must also be acknowledged that the internet and social media have become both a haven and a hunting ground for child predators. These snakes slither through cyberspace, hoping to entice teens for sexual exploitation and abuse.

Cyber predators are extremely shrewd, meticulous, and patient. They will gradually "groom" their intended victims with dialogue meant to cultivate a relationship, including compliments and enticements. Once the teen becomes ensnared, they will pounce—which can take the form of inducing the teen to send them provocative photos that will later be posted or kept in a "private" collection. These photos may also be used later to market the teen if they become trapped in sexual exploitation crimes.

These predators are also not all adults. In May 2017, six New Jersey juveniles—four boys and two girls, ages 13–16—were arrested in connection with hosting social media accounts depicting child pornography or providers of child pornography. The charges include distribution of child pornography, maintaining child pornography/file sharing, possession of child pornography, invasion of privacy, and cyber harassment. The group allegedly coerced girls between the ages of 13–15 to share nude photos that were later posted on social media.

Sometimes, coercion needs not be a factor. Teens will actively engage in sexting, naïvely taking and forwarding suggestive photos of themselves, only to be devastated when these photos appear on social media, especially in the wake of a break-up. There are federal laws that address sexting and exploitation: for example, the Prosecutorial Remedies and Other Tools to end the Exploitation of Children Today (PROTECT) Act of 2003 makes it illegal to produce, distribute, receive, or possess with intent to distribute, any obscene visual depiction of a minor engaged in sexually explicit conduct. Federal law also criminalizes causing a minor to take part in sexually explicit conduct in order to visually depict that conduct. Parents who allow this behavior can also be prosecuted.

Yet federal prosecution of juveniles for sexting may be unlikely. The Federal Juvenile Delinquency Act (FJDA) generally provides that, where possible, juveniles should be prosecuted in state—not federal—courts, making a nationwide change or update in policy unlikely.

STRATEGIES

So, how to prevent a child from coming into contact with the negative aspects of cyberspace?

First and foremost, parents *must* monitor their child's social media accounts and regularly look at what they are sending and receiving. Teens will complain that their privacy is being violated, of course; but to be frank, that's just too bad. *You* are the parent. If something looks suspicious, it is your right and responsibility to immediately intervene.

Some other general net safety guidelines include:

- Limit the time a teen spends on social media. If this means taking their phone or tablet away at a certain point, then so be it.
- Set up parental controls on all devices.

- Review the people your teens are cyber friends with, and review their sites as well as their friend circles to see what kind of behavior they are prone to. Unfriend or block any unwanted access.
- Look for any unexplained behavioral changes in your teen.
- Educate your child on the potential for being stalked by a predator and what some of the warning signs may be.
- Teach the teen to be resilient in the face of adversity, and not be a victim. Be supportive, even if the content is upsetting. This is hard, but empowerment can be a life changer and life saver.
- Find creative uses for social media to help them spend their time online more productively.

Tell your children not to trust anyone, especially if they request suggestive/provocative photos. Invariably, any photos sent will eventually appear on social media, either as a form of bullying or the newly-coined term "sextortion". This is when another party makes a threat to post photos/videos unless the "victim" either pays them or provides sexual favors.

CONCLUSION

It's reasonable to presume that the inventors of the various social media platforms never intended for their platforms be used for harassment, bullying, or criminal purposes. The fact is, however, that they are—daily. Cyberbullying and Cyberbanging have resulted in real consequences, not least of which include suicide and murder. How our society deals with this constantly evolving technology is not so much directly related to the technology itself, which can and should be regulated better (posts encouraging self-harm or criminal behavior should be taken down, etc.) as much as how the targeted individual deals with it. In a later chapter we will discuss the importance of nurturing self-confidence, positive imagery, and coping mechanisms in young people as a means to combat anti-social media behavior, but this is a problem that must be addressed on all involved fronts.

CHAPTER 6

THE MEDIA'S ROLE IN TEEN VIOLENCE

"The important thing is moral choice. Evil has to exist along with good, in order that moral choice may operate. Life is sustained by the grinding opposition of moral entities."

—ANTHONY BURGESS, *A CLOCKWORK ORANGE*

IN AUGUST 2014, eighteen-year-old Michael Brown, an African-American male with a troubled past, was shot and killed by a Ferguson, Missouri police officer. Brown's death sparked an outrage that eventually grew into the Black Lives Matter and Hands Up, Don't Shoot social movements. At the core of the flashpoint incident was a 24-hour media circus, one which was relying heavily on unsubstantiated "eyewitness" accounts and a supposed anti-police agenda. It wasn't long before displays of "hands up" were being seen at demonstrations in the streets and even on the sidelines of professional sporting events.

The Department of Justice's investigation would later find that Brown was the aggressor, not the innocent victim he was initially portrayed to be. The media's depiction of Brown, attempting to be compliant with the officer's demands by raising his hands to surrender but being shot regardless, was based on unreliable witness testimony. The facts later revealed that Brown may have held his hands up at shoulder level briefly, before charging the officer in a threatening manner who responded by shooting him[1].

This incident demonstrates the impact contemporary media has on our social attitudes and behavior. This is not the first nor the last example of the media's role in fomenting a distorted presentation of facts, heedless of the impact this has on our perception of social accountability. Young people were especially caught up in the Ferguson controversy, ignoring the facts of what really happened, and only searching for those slivers of information that validated their reactive behavior.

Another egregious case fueled by an attention-hungry media was the Duke Lacrosse team rape case of March 2006, in which an African-American female stripper accused white members of the Duke lacrosse team of sexually assaulting her. The case was tried in the court of public opinion long before any of those accused stood trial, and innocent lives were ruined as a result of allegations which were later proven to be fabricated. Yet the fact that the alleged victim who lied about the rape, Crystal Mangum, was convicted of second-degree murder in 2013[2], garnered little attention. The media did not appear as interested in reporting this incident, as it would distract or detract from the overall narrative of the Duke Lacrosse case.

Media impacts every facet of our lives, whether in print or online, through entertainment, gaming, social media, etc. There is little that we do, think or say that is not affected by what we see and hear, which we presume to be based in fact, with some socially redeeming value. Unfortunately, in the era of reality television, social media, 24-hour news cycles, smart phones, and political agendas, fact is often a rare commodity. Adolescents, who are not yet physiologically and emotionally developed, are especially vulnerable. Their ability to reason is still developing, which makes discerning fact from fiction difficult, especially when the latter presented as fact. Over the past thirty years, the quality of television programming has deteriorated to such an extent that the concept of age appropriate programming has been all but obliterated. The material that is now presented to teens has desensitized their ability to distinguish the consequences of reality.

ADOLESCENTS AND THE MEDIA

The adolescent demographic is especially vulnerable to the influences of all forms of media due to their still-developing brains, which must struggle to keep up with discernment, interpretation and impulsivity as it is constantly bombarded by stimuli.

The impact of the media on adolescents has been shown to have a profound effect on their self-esteem; for example, in the endless photo spreads of celebrities, which distort an adolescent's perception of how people should look. Television and movies continue to portray a permissive atmosphere of sex—even during prime-time hours. Popular shows such as The Big Bang Theory consistently feature sexual innuendos and overtones; other shows leave little to the imagination. Other shows involving pregnant teens essentially glamorize a phenomenon that was a social stigma in previous generations. There is easy access to pornography on the internet. The media fosters a socially acceptable attitude towards alcohol and even drug use.

Think of it this way: if there were a person in your child's life who espoused these easy-going attitudes towards sex, drugs and alcohol, or acted inappropriately in front of them, would you allow your child to spend time around them? The answer is no; yet they are allowed to indulge this in media.

Regardless, for the purposes of this book it is the impact of the media on violence that we must focus on, an issue that continues to be a great source of concern among parents, law enforcement, teachers, politicians, and child welfare professionals.

When we look at the impact of media on violence among adolescents, we must do so carefully, making sure to examine the issue in its entirety. For example, exposure to depictions of violence does not necessarily equate to an increased propensity toward violence behavior. A violent response, even one with an underlying contribution of violent media, may also be fueled by family discord, substance abuse, mental disease, developmental delays, post-traumatic stress disorder, or peer pressure/bullying. Sound familiar? A child who watches a violent movie is not likely to spontaneously react in a similarly violent fashion in reality but the seeds have been planted.

To a vulnerable teen looking for some form of association, violent movies may be seen as a validation of their plight. *Westside Story* is obviously not an accurate depiction of gang life in New York City, as compared to more compelling gang movies such as *Blood In, Blood Out, American History X, Goodfellas,* and *End of Watch.* These movies don't glorify gang life; rather, they show the actual consequences. Yet there remains that underlying "bad boy" attraction and the aura of excitement surrounding the counter-culture lifestyle depicted in these movies. This is where parents must step in, putting these movies in perspective by teaching their children that while these lifestyles do exist, they are a dangerous and unproductive path to follow.

Aimee Tompkins, in an article for the website Allpsych.com, found that while watching violent television shows children show a twelve percent increase in aggression[3]. She goes on to cite a report by the American Psychological Association which found children may become less sensitive to the pain and suffering of others, may be more fearful of the world around them, and may be more likely to behave in aggressive or hurtful ways toward others when exposed to excessive media violence[4].

The ultimate consequence of these media images is their being replicated in violent acts; the idea that life imitates art. Experts have looked at the impact of violence in movies on influencing real acts of violence, and the results are compelling, though admittedly they represent almost a statistically insignificant percentage of people who actually watch movies. Still, while these acts of violence, such as the massacre in Aurora, Colorado in 2008 during a screening of *The Dark Knight Rises*, are rare, this is no consolation to those families left to grieve dead loved ones, or the survivors who live with permanent physical and emotional scars.

We'll be walking through some of the more compelling instigators of teen violence, such as the emergence of gangsta rap music, violent video games, and how news outlets depict crime, and whether this urges teens to commit copycat crimes and/or suicides.

MUSIC AND MOVIES

To properly appreciate the issues surrounding modern adolescents and the media they are exposed to every minute of every day, there must be some understanding of how we reached this point.

Every generation feels that the younger generation is being exposed to music that may adversely affect their behavior. No era saw this more clearly than the dawn of rock n' roll music, as the hip gyrations of Elvis Presley caused panic attacks among the parents living in the socially puritanical 1950s. Later, it would be the attraction of white teens to African-American performers. Then came the new wave of motorcycle "clubs," with the bad boy biker image created by tight cuffed blue jeans, boots, white T-shirts, and black leather jackets. Parents would be driven apoplectic when answering the door, only to find a Marlon Brando-wannabe waiting to take out their daughter.

Then came the counter-culture sixties: a time for revolution, anti-Vietnam War demonstrations, and an exploding drug culture made socially acceptable by groups such as Jefferson Airplane and the Beatles. As traditional norms were discarded for the emerging culture of, "If it feels good, do it," practicing good parenting became more difficult than ever before.

The hippie countercultural movements of the sixties, which brought with it their mantra of "Sex, Drugs, and Rock N' Roll," was the entry point for many social taboos becoming more accepted into mainstream culture. For much of the 1960s the violent crime rate among teens remained relatively insignificant; there was still a semblance of respect for the law; the tsunami of divorces and single parent households that would soon dominate the family dynamic was yet to occur; parental supervision and the pervasiveness of drugs in communities was in its infancy.

For much of this decade radio, television, with its mere handful of stations, and movies with the emergence of a rating system, were still closely monitored and controlled for content. It was only towards the end of the decade, as the boundaries of free speech began to expand, that media content and language entered new realms. This upheaval would set the stage for the 1970s, a time defined by cities, such as New York, hovering on the verge of bankruptcy, while crime and drug abuse raged out of control.

And yet, the band played on. The 1970s saw the acceptance of recreational drug use and its potential for concurrent addiction reach such heights that President Richard Nixon declared a war on drugs in 1971, and established a dedicated agency in 1973 to address this scourge, the Drug Enforcement Administration. On the silver screen, the new genres of martial arts movies starring Bruce Lee (and their knock-offs) had kids karate chopping everyone and everything in sight, while blaxploitation films such as *Shaft* and *Super Fly* glorified the drug trade and gang life, as well as the violent solutions to problems embraced by the films' heroes.

Violence in films only continued to increase, seeking more and more to capture that "shock value" aesthetic. *A Clockwork Orange, Death Wish, The Texas Chainsaw Massacre;* cult films, but which leave nothing to the imagination as far as gore and depravity are concerned. According to Dr. Peter Hammond, *A Clockwork Orange* was linked to multiple violent crimes and gang rapes, echoing the depictions of same in the film[5].

Outside the film industry, the late seventies also saw the birth of the rap and hip-hop movements, but their melodic rhymes were still relatively benign, and had yet to cross the threshold of advocating violence as we saw emerge in the eighties with the birth of Gangsta Rap. A hard and gritty portrayal of ghetto life now took on a cynical and more violent theme, glorifying gang life, advocating for killing police, and subjugating women as "hoes" and "bitches," which ultimately forced record companies to place parental warning labels on record sleeves, cautioning parents as to the violent content and profane language contained therein. As might be expected, this not only failed to deter purchases, it facilitated them, giving teens an indication of which records were "real" or "hard" enough to warrant listening to.

All of these new forms of media, being used (and misused) in ways completely alien to the experiences of parents at the time, posed an extreme challenge when trying to raise children on the straight and narrow. As far removed as parents were from understanding the attraction and dangers of violent music and film, their challenges were nothing compared to what awaited them in the digital age.

VIDEO GAMES

I spent more than a decade reporting on the drug-fueled violence in Ciudad Juarez, Mexico, just across the border from El Paso, Texas. Cd. Juarez has been one of the most violent cities in the world for most of the new millennium; while the insatiable American appetite for drugs has caused death and carnage across the entire country, Cd. Juarez remains the flashpoint—at one time things were so bad it garnered the moniker, "Murder Capital of the World". So, you can imagine my surprise when I came across the video game *Call of Juarez: The Cartel* (2011), a game which featured the area and its difficulties prominently.

In poverty-stricken Mexico, the attraction of cartel life for teens is virtually insurmountable. Fast and easy money draws thousands of teens into the ranks of the country's various cartels. The attraction is also fueled by the glamour of *corridos*—folk songs which glorify cartel life and personalities such as El Chapo Guzman, as well as images of gold-plated weapons, jewelry, and beautiful women. (This is not just a Mexico problem; tens of thousands of teens in the U.S. with direct ties to Mexico face a similar dilemma. An official in one southern New Mexico school district that draws students from nearby Mexico said some of them are already involved in the cartels and working their way up by smuggling drugs into the school.)

The given description for *Call of Juarez: The Cartel* goes as follows: "When a Mexican drug cartel bombs a U.S. law enforcement agency, the U.S. government puts together a special task force to hunt them down. Play as Ben McCall, a brutal LAPD cop and descendent of Ray McCall, or Eddie Guerra, a DEA agent with a chronic gambling habit, or gang-affiliated street kid turned FBI agent, Kim Evans. As you dig into the mystery of the bombing and fight to dismantle the cartel, you'll embark on a blood-soaked road trip through California, Arizona, New Mexico, Texas, and, ultimately, Juarez, Mexico." The timing and content of this game could not be worse, as violence continues to grip Cd. Juarez, forcing many of its residents to move to the U.S.—including vulnerable teens who might see this game as one more enticement to emulate this lifestyle.

Nor is *Call of Juarez: The Cartel* an outlier. The *Grand Theft Auto* game franchise, one of the most successful game series ever developed, features police depicted as racist thugs, frontal nudity of main characters, and a scoring system which assigns point values for committing crimes. There are even games which not only depict the horror of a school shooting; they place the player in control of the shooter, structuring gameplay around locating and killing one's digital classmates.

One such game, *Active Shooter* by Revived Games and developed by Acid, garnered media attention after the outrage surrounding the game's premise led to its being removed from digital storefronts like Steam, an online retailer that distributes games. The game, which was removed prior to its official release, gave players the opportunity to be either a shooter or a SWAT team member, and the choice between a school or office scenario. Despite the game offering players the options between playing a "good guy" or "bad guy," there can be no doubt that a teen who is legitimately considering a similar act of violence could have used this game as a virtual training tool to build up their resolve.

While the game was pulled before being distributed, the point is that things should never have reached this point. Even the thought of someone using a school shooting as a form of entertainment should be nauseating, yet it demonstrates how unscrupulous people will go to any lengths to capitalize on a tragic real-life trend.

The danger in a product like this is in the sense of validation and social acceptance it can foster. Many teens are unable to properly distinguish fantasy from reality, an attitude which can serve both as a catalyst for the violence we see from this demographic, as well as the desensitization towards violence. In reality, there are no "extra lives"; victims really do die, and the criminals really do go to jail. Yet this continued bombardment of violent games makes it extremely difficult to avoid these temptations, especially in the absence of parental guidance.

Researchers have found increased levels of aggression among teens who play extended bouts of violent video games. Bruce Bartholow, associate professor of psychology in the College of Arts and

Science at the University of Missouri-Columbia, says, "More than any other media, these video games encourage active participation in violence. From a psychological perspective, video games are excellent teaching tools because they reward players for engaging in certain types of behavior. Unfortunately, in many popular video games, the behavior is violence."[6] Bartholow concluded that players become less responsive to violence, and this diminished brain response predicts an increase in aggression.[7]

A 2014 article in the Journal of the American Medical Association[8] described how researchers studied 3,034 adolescents over three years of playing violent video games. They found that playing violent video games did increase long-term aggressive behavior by producing general changes in how participants perceived aggressive behavior.

The examples given here comprise an extremely short list of what our children are exposed to for hours on end in the name of entertainment. Despite how much fun teens may have with these materials, research shows that violence in media *does* impact violence in reality. Granted, as with other acts of teen violence, the act of playing the game itself is only one piece of a destructive puzzle, and may not be the sole driving force to commit violence.

While it is somewhat outside the scope of this discussion, the increasingly sedentary American lifestyle may also be somewhat to blame for the ill effects of violent video games. There are a staggering number of children playing video games with no outlet, such as exercise or team sports, to let them decompress from their gaming experiences, to burn off energy and aggression in healthful, directed ways. When children choose not to participate in physical activity, which is necessary for their proper growth and development, it is a parental failure. More than just placing violent media in its proper context, it is the responsibility of parents to ensure that the intake of media itself is done as part of a well-rounded and enriching lifestyle.

NEWS MEDIA AND SOCIAL AWARENESS

Despite access to an overabundance of 24-hour news and internet outlets, today's adolescents are disturbingly out of touch with social, cultural, economic and public safety issues, as well as the impact of current events. Try asking a seventeen-year-old who the vice president is, or who the U.S. fought in World War II, or to name the three branches of government. More often than not, their only reply will be a glazed look (or an immediate move towards the nearest smartphone). The new millennium's attitude to "news" is one steeped in public opinion based on social media, with more regard given to reality television than reality itself. Discernment between fact and opinion is obfuscated, and subject to a host of agendas and a move towards value through entertainment.

Adolescents are learning from the media that appropriate social discourse and debate are not acceptable behavior, that being heard means being the loudest and most disruptive voice. Real life examples of this abound: the campus revolts in Berkley against free speech; the call for abolishing Immigration and Customs Enforcement; the Black Lives Matter movement; or demonstrators screaming at government officials in restaurants. These are just a few of the images that teens are bombarded with, which are now seen as "acceptable" behavior when you disagree with someone. But it isn't, or shouldn't be, acceptable; it should be seen for the anti-social behavior it clearly is.

So, how does this impact the issue of violence among teens? One trend that can't be ignored is the ostensible impact of the media on copycat violence. The data shows how frequently this occurs. Impressionable teens who hunger for attention see a chance for their five minutes of infamy and decide that death outweighs a lifetime of anonymity. This is especially relevant with school shootings, which receive constant coverage for hours and days on end. Is it important that the public be informed in these cases? Absolutely; but we also cannot ignore the potential impact on teens contemplating similar acts of violence. Some stations have started opting not to identify shooters as a means of mitigating the extent of this sought-after attention. A study found that twenty to thirty percent of such attacks are inspired by previous incidents, especially those extensively covered by the media[9]. The researchers said, "Several past studies have found that media reports of suicides and homicides appear to subsequently increase the incidence of similar events in the community, apparently due to the coverage planting the seeds of ideation in at-risk individuals to commit similar acts."[10]

Sociologist Zeynep Tufekci finds a distinct impact of extended media coverage of mass shootings on copycat incidents, especially when it is manifested through an existing mental illness: "As a sociologist, I am increasingly concerned that the tornado of media coverage that swirls around each such mass killing, and the acute interest in the identity and characteristics of the shooter—as well as the detailed and sensationalist reporting of the killer's steps just before and during the shootings—may be creating a vicious cycle of copycat effects similar to those found in teen and other suicides."[11]

He makes the following recommendations to help mitigate copycat acts of violence[12]:

1. Law enforcement should not release details of the methods and manner of the killings, and those who learn those details should not share them.

2. If and when social media accounts of the killers are located, law enforcement should work with the platforms to immediately pull them.

3. The name of the killer should not be revealed immediately.

4. The intense push to interview survivors and loved ones in their most vulnerable moments should be stopped.

STRATEGIES

Parenting a teenager is one of the most difficult stages of child rearing. Rarely will you be seen as right in their eyes; rarely is a suggestion made without some kind of dissent or argument being the response. Changes in identity, raging hormones, their environment, and emerging stressors all contribute to the ups and downs of a teen's personality.

This is when what I like to call strategic parenting comes in. It is a fruitless effort to totally ban something from a teen, especially as they perceive themselves to be adults (or at least adult-like). If you have a strong enough foundation of discipline in the home, by all means go for it; the problem is, with both parents typically working, teenagers will seek other forms of structure as a replacement, be it social media, video games, television and film, or music. It is very likely that they will rebel and, whatever you may restrict from them, they will do anyway, or else search out another, perhaps more antagonizing activity.

Under no circumstances should antisocial or rebellious behavior be ignored, of course. Ignoring these behaviors or treating them as "just a phase" is just as detrimental when it comes to establishing disciplined behavior. The first step in addressing media, regardless of what form it takes, is to either listen to or play it yourself to see what your child is involved in. What is the content and what are its the potential consequences? Talk to your teen; ask them what they are getting out of the medium in terms of entertainment value. This is a good way to start a dialogue. Discuss with them the consequences of the medium, and what needs to be addressed and why. If the media is violent, perhaps discuss real-life instances of violence and the impact it has on people. Hopefully, this can help ground the teen's experiences somewhat, enabling them to take a broader perspective on what starts as an abstract.

This may not always fly, but it is a good way to establish a constructive dialogue with your teen. Inevitably, you may still need to consider separating your child from the medium, especially if they manifest reflective behavior.

Like any other immersive or emotionally affective activity, children can become addicted to video games. If this occurs, know that just like any addiction, going cold turkey is hard. Consider options to wean the child off the game. This can be as simple as making time to actually spend with them or encourage them to find an alternative activity, be it sports, art, hobbies, or any other area of interest they may have to serve as a diversion. Place time limits on how long they play, if such things can be enforced. Make it a negotiation; this empowers the teen to make their own constructive decisions.

There are dozens of other strategies online to explore when addressing any concerns involving video game addiction. The key, however, is to start a dialogue with your teen in a constructive fashion rather than a punitive act such as removing the game (although that may be necessary if all else fails).

CONCLUSION

It's inescapable—electronic media is an integral part of our lives. What is still up for debate, however, is how this media is to be used. Music, television, movies, and video games all have an incredible influence on adolescent behavior. It is up to parents to monitor the habits of their children and note any concurrent behavioral changes that may serve as warning flags, such as social disassociation, anger, substance abuse, etc. Parents must limit the time their children spend on video games and encourage alternate constructive activities that allow for well-rounded physical, emotional, and cognitive development.

The long and short of it is that teens need to be exposed more to current events and how it impacts their lives and those of others. Exploring the perspectives of different news outlets and how information fits within the values you want to instill in your child is the best way to broaden their perspective. This will empower them to make more informed decisions in the future based on fact rather than emotion. Allow them to debate you if they disagree with your position. This can be frustrating, but this engagement allows parents to at least see what their child is thinking. Teach them to gather all the information they can before determining what perspective makes more sense to them. Teach them the value of debate based on facts not emotions. Teach respect for others and for differing opinions. In these cases, the value of debate and compromise, not out-screaming each other, can't be over-estimated. Through this, they will find new opportunities for emotional growth—and so will you.

CHAPTER 7

TARNISHED PARTICIPATION TROPHIES: THE NEED FOR SELF-RESILIENCE

"I don't measure a man's success by how high he climbs but how high he bounces when he hits bottom."
—General George S. Patton

URING THE MID-1970S there was a growing movement among physical educators to increase participation of all students. As a result, activities were modified to provide an equal playing field where all could participate free of scrutiny and judgement. At the time, both my wife and I were in college majoring in physical education. We came from the dodgeball and rope climbing generation. I could never make it to the ceiling of the gym on that darn rope and was forced to watch as my friends scampered to the top like pirates on a ship's mast. I took my share of ribbing, of course, but I moved on and found activities I did excel in. As for dodgeball, I took as many shots to the head as I gave, but when I went home to tell my parents, there was no outcry or pity—it was all part of the challenges of growing up. Children were expected to deal with and learn from the physical and emotional pain and move on.

The rise of the "everyone's a winner" mentality gave way to a unique era, not only in sports but in the physical and emotional development of an entire generation. The concept of results and excellence on the playing field or court were traded out for inclusion, feeling good, and having fun—no winners or losers. Losing in sports is an anathema; self-esteem preservation is tantamount; all children have equal attributes, the thought goes, and therefore deserve an award just for showing up—the ubiquitous participation trophy.

Raising four children, all of whom were involved in multiple sports throughout their school years, I sat through many awards banquets. From my seat, I could see the downsides of "leveling the playing field." Most of the kids who felt driven to work hard continued to work hard; the ones who didn't became more complacent, because their effort was already validated with an award. There was no longer an inspiration for self-improvement, discipline, or sacrifice.

Advocates of full inclusion and equal playing time for all ignore the adverse impact this has had on childhood resiliency, which in turn has consequences for how these children deal with adversity. In worst case scenarios, this lack of resiliency, especially when faced with a physical or emotional challenge (i.e. bullying) has resulted in violent responses against oneself or others.

Rather than extol the benefits of hard work and overcoming adversity, we've taught a generation of children to be complacent and feel victimized if they get their feelings hurt. These children (who are now parents) were raised to think that winning isn't important—that having fun is, that everyone gets to play, regardless of their abilities and the impact on the outcome. We have given rise to the so-called Snowflake Generation where safe spaces and therapy dogs are now available on college campuses. But the fact is there are winners and losers in real life; just showing up does not warrant a management track position in your first week of employment.

Ashley Merryman wrote in the *New York Times*, "When children make mistakes, our job should not be to spin those losses into decorated victories. Instead, our job is to help kids overcome setbacks, to help them see that progress over time is more important than a particular win or loss, and to help them graciously congratulate the child who succeeded when they failed"[1]. She goes on to say that, "When it comes to rewards, people argue that kids must be treated identically: everyone must always win. That is misguided. And there are negative outcomes. Not just for specific children, but for society as a whole."[2]

Dr. Vivian Diller wrote in *Psychology Today* that real life (not reality TV) requires a pragmatic approach that is dictated by the ebbs and flows of success and failure, and that the latter is merely part of the developmental process. If this is eliminated by parents glossing over losses directly impacts the child's resilience and ability to problem solve for future setbacks—ones that actually count in life, that involve jobs or relationships, things more important than the outcome of a youth soccer game. When you come home from a long day at work where everything went wrong, there won't be a cheerleader squad of parents waiting for you to congratulate you on a great day. "Life is not divided into semesters. You don't get summers off and very few employers are interested in helping you find yourself. Do that on your own time."[3]

This becomes a major conundrum for parents. How much should parents try to protect and shield their children from the real world? At what point does it actually become detrimental to their future ability to face adversity? Nobody likes to see their child hurt or disappointed, and the natural first reaction is to try and fix it. But we forget how resilient children inherently are—that is, until the adults mess it up. Most kids will face a loss on the field or a bad grade and ultimately move on. The trend towards blaming others, be it a coach, a teacher, or a member of their peer group, is a learned behavior, one they absorb from parents who see the initial hurt and think it will not subside quickly enough and that their aggressive intervention to make things right is the solution. Most kids will shrug a loss off, more focused on making plans to be with their friends later that day—until they see how upset their parents are over the loss or the "bad reffing."

This is where we get into another syndrome that directly impacts a child's behavior: some may call it the Little League parent, or hockey mom, but however it is referred to, it describes the irrational behavior of parents on the sidelines of games who ultimately resort to violence against coaches, referees, or the parents of the opposing team. Incidents like these have risen exponentially in the past ten years, to the point where youth leagues essentially have parents sign a waiver ensuring they will act like adults while their children play. Now consider the indelible mark made on a child's psyche when they are playing a game and out of the corner of their eyes they see a group of parents fighting on the sideline, getting in the face of a referee, or even resorting to violence.

For the peewee level athlete, they may learn to see this as acceptable behavior, since they saw their parent behave in such boorish fashion. If they are displeased with the outcome of an authority figure, seeing their parent strike a coach or referee sends the dangerous message that, "It was in the heat of the game," will be taken as a legitimate excuse for their actions. Yet we are shocked when these kids grow into incorrigible teens, who back talk or even attack teachers and classmates.

This sense of entitlement, begun in the 1970s and passed down through the following generations, has created nothing short of a monster. The correlation of youth violence to the presumption that children who cannot cope with adversity will ultimately snap is admittedly anecdotal. We also want to avoid making broad, generational assumptions in terms of upbringing and lasting effects. But what we can't ignore is the totality of what we are seeing in terms of youth violence in the streets and schools. Consider the teen who contemplates or commits suicide because they cannot cope with the pressure of being bullied or ostracized. Bullying is an unfortunate element for some in their growth process; most kids do get bullied at one point or another. On the other side, there are children who are raised in an environment where everything turns out well in the end, who are shocked to find out that life—especially for most teens—can suck. Are these issues profound enough to cause someone to end their life? Most of the time, it is not, but these teens don't see it any other way. They don't, or *can't*, see a solution because of poor coping skills development.

In fact, very rarely do we teach our children active problem solving. We teach them that if scenario A happens, do this; if scenario B occurs, do this, leaving them with no framework to fall back on should solution A or B fail to work the first time.

We need to put more effort into teaching children coping and stress management skills. Avoid turning every defeat into a false victory and treat it rather as a teachable moment. You can still be a supportive parent and put your arm around your child, but at the same time tell them what went wrong and what the options are for how it can be prevented in the future. There are more lessons to be learned from defeat than success; losing gives you the opportunity to strive for a goal. As an athlete, I often heard from coaches, "That was a good loss". I could never understand why a coach would say this, but as I grew older I finally understood: a "good loss" is one which allows you to avoid complacency after a series of victories. It allows you to stay attentive to detail and task. It also injects humility, diluting arrogance. It allows you to further improve. All of which are valuable life skills.

We must also learn to recognize the risks of indulging our children. Any reasonable parent wants the best for their child, to give them what they never had. Trying to keep them socially connected through current fashion and technology trends, sports equipment, camps…the list is endless.

The danger is when this indulging turns into enabling. The stage of enabling is when a child expects rather than asks for and earns something. When they fail to get what they want, their reaction can range from pitiful sulking to an outright tantrum. Then, in order to resolve the crisis, the parent concedes, and the cycle continues, eventually escalating into higher demands.

Rather than concede, giving up just to appease your child, this is when parents need to put their proverbial foot down and tell the child that their request cannot be fulfilled. More importantly, tell them why; is it because their request for purchasing something means the difference between you paying a utility bill or not? Parents need to stand their ground and realize that they will not always be there to pick up the pieces for their child. If they grow up to be ill-prepared for life's challenges because you did everything for them, and they are unable to solve problems without an emotional meltdown, you have not made your child happy; you have done them a disservice as a parent.

A tragic example of poor coping skills compounded by mental illness occurred in Jacksonville, Florida. On August 26, 2018, David Katz, 24, of Baltimore opened fire at a Madden football video game tournament, killing two and wounding nine after he lost a game that eliminated him from the tournament. Katz took his own life after the rampage. Katz, an obsessive gamer, had a troubled adolescence and was reportedly twice hospitalized for psychiatric issues and prescribed antipsychotic and antidepressant medications.

There are also those parents who attempt to fix their child's misgivings in school through inappropriate intervention with teachers. This typically occurs when students fail to do their homework, or have "too much" homework, or receive detention for a violation of a school policy or a behavioral issue in the classroom. According to the parent, this is always the teacher's fault, that their child would never behave like that. As a result, there is no sense of accountability, and this learned behavior can carry over into tragedy.

Consider the notorious 2013 "Affluenza" case of sixteen-year-old Ethan Couch, who killed four people while driving drunk with a blood alcohol level three times the legal limit. He alleges that his rich parents never taught him right from wrong, and despite facing more than twenty years in prison, his defense attorney convinced the judge not to send him to prison, but to instead walk away with ten years' probation as a juvenile offender. This only further facilitates Couch's attitude towards responsibility: "He never learned that sometimes you don't get your way," says Couch's court appointed psychologist, Gary Miller[4]. The story ends as you might expect: in 2015 Couch, with the assistance of his enabling mother, violated his probation and fled to Mexico where he was arrested and extradited back to the U.S.

THE CASE FOR HEROES

I've always been a history buff, and frequently refer to the words of famous people who were successful in the face of great adversity. Unfortunately, our education system eschews our national heroes for a variety of reasons, in a time when children need inspiration to excel and deal with adversity on their own more than ever. This chapter opens with the words of World War II General George S. Patton, who tells us that it's OK to fail, that in fact it is human nature. What defines an individual is how they recover, learn from their mistakes and move on. If we don't teach this to today's entitled society of complainers and entitled expectations, we cannot be surprised when they fail to succeed.

My personal hero is Teddy Roosevelt, a man who was never short of inspirational speeches, and who more importantly practiced what he preached. Despite being born into a wealthy family, Roosevelt worked doggedly his entire life, whether as a politician, rancher, chief of the NYPD, a Rough Rider, or an author. His life was defined by success and failure, but he never made excuses or gave up. "Nothing in this world is worth having or worth doing unless it means effort, pain, difficulty." This triumvirate of personal virtue is something that our modern society could do with a lot more of.

I often refer to a line from Tom Hanks in the movie *A League of their Own*, when Geena Davis' character has decided to quite the women's baseball team. He says, "Quitting, you'll regret this for the rest of your life." She then says it was just getting too hard, leading to Hanks' memorable reply: "It's *supposed* to be hard. If it wasn't hard, everyone would do it. The hard is what makes it great."

POOR COPING SKILLS AND VIOLENCE

The World Health Organization draws a direct link between poor life skills and violence among children[5], something I see daily at the adult detention center I work in. There is an underlying ambivalence to others which manifests in acts of violence, some of which are unspeakable. The WHO identifies the pillars of coping with everyday life as *cognitive, emotional, interpersonal* and *social*. Being brought up in an environment where these traits are lacking will likely put an adolescent on the fast track for criminal behavior, as they come to see this behavior as normal.

Researchers have found that being exposed to violence, both as a witness and as a victim, can have a direct impact on the commission of violence by adolescents[6]. This strongly supports the role of environment in the potential for violence. Look at what is occurring on the streets of Chicago, where warring gangs have laid siege to the city. The violence perpetrated by teen members of MS-13 comes as no surprise once we consider the historic culture of violence in El Salvador, where just a generation ago there were death squads and children forced into military service by both sides of a civil war that raged for more than a decade. These experiences leave an indelible mark that is hard to erase.

However, while the task may be daunting, there *is* hope for appropriate socialization of children and the prevention of violence. Among the various strategies shown to be effective are:

Feelings and Physiological Arousal

This training helps form the basis for the subsequent principles. There is scant data as to how many children are exposed to trauma and the resultant impact this will have on future behavior.

Understanding the stages of victimization is important to put this in context. There is a misunderstanding that an individual has to personally experience the wrath of a violent act in order to be traumatized, but this is not the case. Trauma can manifest itself in the following ways:

Primary victimization. This is when the individual is the victim of an attack. This can take the form of physical, emotional, or sexual abuse in the home or being victimized by violence at school or in the streets. This will have the most profound impact on the child who will have physical and emotional scars. Many of the women at my jail were sexually abused as children which resulted in low self-esteem that fueled subsequent drug abuse.

Secondary victimization. Here the child observes an act of violence but is not necessarily a victim. Nevertheless, they will still be traumatized. With the violence sweeping Chicago in recent years, it is very difficult for children in already depressed economic areas to escape the impact violence has on their life. From the ubiquitous police car lights and sirens to crime scene tape to wailing family members desperate to get word of their murdered loved ones, the strain is overwhelming.

Tertiary victimization. The child is detached from the violent scene but relates to the incident either because they knew the victim or were empathetic with victims in their age demographic. This is fueled by the aforementioned media saturation, especially when the incident is particularly violent. This can be felt among students nationwide in the wake of a school shooting or on a more micro level when a classmate dies.

These stages all feed into post-traumatic stress disorder, which in turn results in a multitude of behavioral issues that neither the child, parents, or teachers fully link to the experience. Therefore, counseling should be implemented immediately. Of the most compelling signs/symptoms that could contribute to teen violence is impulsive, aggressive/hostile behavior, and anxiety[7]. These may cause the teen to lash out at the slightest provocation.

I N 2012, I had the opportunity to speak to a student at a prominent Catholic high school in El Paso, Texas. The student, like many of his classmates, came from an affluent family in nearby Ciudad Juarez, the "Murder Capital of the World" at the time. He described a near-kidnapping experience he'd had, as well as seeing two men shot to death in the middle of the street execution-style.

He was not alone in these experiences. To address this, the school provided a class in victimization just so the students could understand the emotions that were surfacing. The class was also attended by American students who feared for their friends coming across the border. The student said the program provided a better understanding of the anxiety and anger he was exhibiting.

Imagine the tens of thousands of unaccompanied youths coming into the United States from Central America. Not only do they endure (and hope to escape) violence in their home country, they have to survive a treacherous journey through Mexico, experience the apprehension at the border and subsequent placement with a relative, most of whom they've never met, in a community that is foreign to them—creating the perfect conditions for PTSD to set it. These children become recruiting fodder for MS-13 or become victims themselves. There are few resources available to these children once they are placed, yet communities wonder why they are seeing a rise in violence from this gang.

STRATEGIES

Using Distraction and Relaxation Techniques

Once a trauma-induced disorder is identified, teaching the child how to cope with it to prevent a violent reaction is a major stepping stone.

Among the various techniques available, one of the most productive is through the use of distraction and relaxation. The foundation for this must be laid by a mental health professional but can and should be continued to be exercised by the individual on their own. Similar to pharmacologic interventions, compliance and consistency is crucial to a successful intervention.

Distraction techniques. As the name implies, distraction techniques are used to deflect the brain from obsessing over a stressor, such as memories of a traumatic event that may serve as a trigger for a violent reaction. As complex as the brain is, it can only really focus on one thing at a time. Encourage activities the teen enjoys or getting together with friends. Emphasis must be placed on not giving the teen an opportunity to wallow in trauma which can be detrimental to their well-being.

Relaxation techniques. For adolescents that need to take a step back from life to regroup before making a drastic decision or committing a drastic act, learning to relax is key. For starters, teens at risk of high levels of anxiety *must* avoid stimulants such as tobacco, energy drinks, colas and sugary sodas. These are laden with caffeine and sugar and counteract the body's attempts to relax. Obviously stimulant-type drugs should be avoided, as should depressants, which the teen might naively think will help them safely relax. One technique is to lay in a comfortable position and go to your "happy place", visualizing a tranquil or positive experience while slowly inhaling and exhaling. Listening to sounds such as waves or rainfall can also be incorporated. Encourage the teen to engage as many of their senses as possible, to try to even smell what they are visualizing. It's amazing what can be accomplished when there are no distractions. It must be emphasized that this takes practice; don't let the teen give up after one attempt. This can be done throughout the day; the longer the better, but even repeated short bouts may get them calmly through the day.

Developing Problem-Solving Skills

For many teens, developing problem-solving skills goes hand-in-hand with self-control. Crises pop up constantly; how these are dealt with will be based on the teen's prior exposure to problem/conflict resolution. If a teen grew up seeing their parents or adults reacting to problems through violence or substance abuse, they will likely see this as the natural course to take. The teen must be taught how to take a step back and analyze the situation. Teach them to ask, 'How will this problem affect me personally, physically, or financially currently and in the future?' Is the problem catastrophic, or is it a short-term issue that will be resolved in time or through open dialogue? What options do I have in the meantime time to live through the problem before it can be resolved? What resources are available to solve the problem? These are all questions the teen needs to be asked, then given a systematic approach to determining the reasonable response.

Problem solving will become an invaluable tool for the teen as they get older. They will not always have a doting parent to enable them or a social worker to facilitate them. At some point they will be on their own and have to deal with real life. If violence or substance abuse is all they were exposed to, then they need to be taught the consequences of these options and how they do nothing for their plight. Most of the time, they know that nothing good comes out of these negative coping mechanisms, because they lived through the negative consequences. They just need to be shown the constructive options.

Self-Control

Impulse control is not a strong quality among teens, and this lack of self-control is what contributes to a large percentage of youth violence. Some of it is environmentally learned behavior, while some of it can be the result of a mental disability. We see substance experimentation turn into addiction, reactive behavior turn to violence (usually over irrelevant details), attacks on other teens for wearing the colors of a rival gang—even if they weren't in that gang to begin with.

The American Psychological Association[7] suggests controlling anger responses by first identifying the trigger that is setting the teen off. This can be done through a series of exercises where they make a list of things that cause them to erupt into fits of anger. Once the trigger is recognized, the next step is to try to step away from the anger trigger and do relaxation techniques. This can be difficult for a teen who may fear they will lose street credibility by walking away from a confrontation, but if they can be taught to appreciate the consequences better, this may be less of a challenge. The APA also suggests not dwelling on the anger trigger. However, it is dealt with, teens must be taught to move on, rather than continue to let the trigger affect them. This may be easier said than done, especially when reputations are on the line, which is why it is better to have this as part of a regular lesson inserted in all facets of school life. High-risk teens need to be shown alternative behavior to adversity to violence.

Self-Awareness

One of the biggest challenges for today's teens is personal identity. As they attempt to transition, both physically and emotionally, into their developing body, their feeling is one of, "I look like an adult but I'm not quite sure how to act like one." This internal conflict can manifest itself in violent behavior if not identified and appropriately channeled. Compounding this risk element are other external factors already described, such as domestic discord, bullying, drugs and alcohol.

This adolescent angst must be identified and channeled constructively. The teen must identify their perceived strengths and attributes as an individual. Ask them: how do *they* see themselves? Teens have to be coached to be able to do this, especially if they already possess a negative image of themselves brought on by a perceived physical shortcoming such as obesity. Even worse are cases where parents have directly attacked the child's self-worth, saying they were a mistake and how they wished the child was never born. This can be an insurmountable obstacle for any child to overcome. Add in the additional pressures from peers and this can be a recipe for either suicide or an active shooter incident.

Defining and developing acceptable behavior to interact productively in society is critical for any individual, teens included. However, many people—especially teens during their rebellious periods—perceive this as surrendering their individuality. This is not necessarily true; maintaining individual uniqueness is completely acceptable, so long as it does not infringe on the rights of others or interferes with your potential for employment or educational opportunities. Some of the world's most creative people were social outcasts until their contributions were better appreciated, usually after their death.

In order to cultivate this type of awareness, a teen must have a proper understanding of what society expects of them. All too often we see teens going for a job interview wearing a T-shirt, torn jeans and sneakers, answering questions in street slang. This is not going to win over an employer; yet because of the unrealistic expectations instilled in teens by the participation trophy mentality, teens overestimate their value and assume they are owed a job, an opportunity, a promotion. This is just as much about social responsibility as it is social awareness. There are differences in expected behavior for different social encounters; knowing this can greatly benefit a teen.

Relationship Building

Many teens who are prone to violence have poor interpersonal skills. Often, they live in dysfunctional families where this is perceived as normal. But proper social skills such as interactive conversational and listening skills form the basis of good relationship building, as does trust and loyalty. Granted, there is no such thing as a real Brady Bunch homelife; every family experiences some form of dysfunction or another. What matters is how prevalent it is, as that is what will affect the children.

Relationships form the basis for a civilized society. Major elements of a good relationship include compromise, listening, sharing, self-sacrifice, contributing, and controlling negative emotions; anger and confrontation serve no purpose. Children who experience physical and emotional domestic violence know what they are seeing occur in their home is wrong, but may find themselves acting out the same behavior when they are in a relationship, even as teens. They can only act on what they know, and all they know is what they see every day. If they don't experience good relationships, they can't know how to have a good relationship.

Setting Goals

What does your teen want out of life, both now and in the future? How do they see themselves achieving their goals? The typical teen rarely looks beyond a year or two; in some depressed communities, life is measured day by day. Reaching their sixteenth birthday without being shot, stabbed, or killed is a common goal for many teens in the new America. We need to teach our teens what life has to offer, both within and outside the confines of their communities. As tough as some teens may seem, most are afraid of cutting the umbilical cord and losing the familiarity of their neighborhood. In their mind they may be the big fish where they currently live, and moving would disrupt their level of street credibility and influence. Why disrupt that by setting a goal that would cause them to leave, even if it is for a better life?

There may not be anything wrong with setting short and long-term goals for school or employment by staying in their community. If the individual is a troubled teen who has broken their destructive cycle, they will be an invaluable resource to other teens by being a role model, showing others that it is possible to live a violence-free life.

Goals must be specific, realistic and attainable. It is incumbent on adults, be they teachers, social workers, or parents, to provide teens with the resources to achieve their goals—on their own, obstacles and all. It is important for the adults to remember that it is the teen's goal and not theirs. Their role is as goal facilitators, not definers, who may want to establish a goal for the teen they themselves wanted and didn't achieve in their younger days. Demonstrating how to fill out a job application, how to dress, and how to speak during an interview is one approach. What are the local options for employment? Is the military a viable option to escape their environment while learning discipline and a skill? There is no shortage of options; they just need to be pointed out, especially if the teen comes from a home dominated by despair. Despair is a horrible obstacle to overcome; they need to see they can overcome whatever real or perceived obstacles they face.

Responsible Decision-Making

Many of the inmates I work with have repeatedly told me they are in their predicament because they made bad choices in life. Whether it was drugs, alcohol, or criminal behavior, most say they were never given the tools to make sound decisions and were left to fend for themselves.

Bad choices are often the product of peer pressure and poor adult guidance, itself a major contributor to adolescent behavior. Teens have this sense of invincibility; we've all experienced it, and most of us have done extremely stupid things in our younger days that leave us scratching our gray hair today, wondering how we ever avoided serious consequences.

One very extreme end of the spectrum is the teen who was brought up exposed to family or friends who were involved in criminal enterprises. To them, the consequence of jail is not seen as a punishment but a rite of passage, one which demonstrates to the homies that they have proven themselves and deserve street credibility. Unfortunately, in many gang-infested communities, this is the pinnacle of existence.

Part of this process is teaching teens to weigh the cost-benefits of their decisions. If I do this, what will the consequences be? These can be financial, emotional, legal, etc. What will the benefits be? The problem is that adolescent invincibility rarely allows for consideration of consequences. There will be that teen whose friends say try heroin just once, because it feels good and you can stop at any time; or, have one more drink at the party. Something as simple as taking a sheet of paper and making a cost and benefit columns and having the teen fill in what they perceive as appropriate for each side is a fundamental exercise.

THE ROLE OF RESPONSIBLE ADULTS

The question we must ask, after discussing what must be done to help properly acclimate our teens to a life of success, is who is going to teach these valuable lessons? There would seem to be no shortage of resources, such as parents, educators, and social workers, yet each has proven to be inadequate in getting these messages across in well-publicized catastrophic cases. Behavioral norms and expectations have eroded to the lowest common denominators in an attempt at social parity. We no longer strive to be the best because we don't want to offend anyone. Yet real life is a Darwinian competition, and failure to acknowledge this does no one any favors.

So, what other recourse is there? The typical go-to is the parents, but this may not always be feasible. There may be family dysfunction, which does little good, or the parents may have to work long hours just to make ends meet. Regardless of whether it is their responsibility, teachers are among the only ones left who can incorporate these techniques into their curricula. Thankfully, this is not only possible, it requires very little effort on the part of the educators, as all of these are basic life skills a teacher should have anyway when working with children.

Another option, albeit an unpopular one, is mandatory parenting classes for parents whose children have been arrested for low to mid-level crimes. These children still have a chance, but not if their environment refuses to change. I'll be the first to admit that there is no such thing as a perfect parent; we all make mistakes and learn as we go. But we *can* learn from the example of others—as long as they are positive examples. So, if a child is charged with a crime, part of the process should be to understand why they did it and what can be done to remedy any deficiency at home that may have caused it.

Participation in these programs should involve both the parent and **teen**, especially if the former is the problem and there is a dysfunctional family cycle that needs to be broken. If this is not feasible, educators can still implement these strategies in classrooms through specific goal setting and behavioral expectations that are then enforced.

This may be a drastic, even unrealistic measure but what are the alternatives if a child is not put on the right track? Jail, even juvenile detention, is not a productive environment for youth development; you do not want children taught skill sets by criminals. That marks the start of a cycle there may be no escape from.

CONCLUSION

Most teens are inadequately prepared to face real-world challenges. The Participation Trophy concept that they were raised on—this idea that there are no winners and losers and that everyone equally contributes to the effort—couldn't be further from how the real-world works. When most teens are confronted with adversity they are at a loss for how to react appropriately. To some, suicide appears to be their only option to escape whatever is bothering them. Others lash out violently against others. We must walk the fine line between caring for, indulging and enabling our children and providing them with the coping skills to face adversity.

By the same token, parents and educators need to recognize the impact of traumatic experiences on children. Unfortunately, violence is a fact of life for this generation like never before. School shootings, gang violence, and domestic violence are much more prevalent than in previous generations. While it is unimaginable for us to experience any of this as a young person, we still need to provide coping skills after the incident has occurred, as well as response mechanisms that better empower our teens in the face of adversity. Crisis management skills can help to alleviate some of the post-incident trauma because there is a greater sense of control over the situation.

The need for resiliency cannot be overstated. As mentioned earlier, I am a history buff, and make a point of appreciating the lessons of those who have led impactful lives. One such person is Navy SEAL Marcus Luttrell. His experiences, which served as the basis for the film *Lone Survivor* (2013), proudly reflects the ethos of the Navy SEALs. His story is one of survival in the face of adversity and a testament to how resilience helps us to overcome challenges. And while most of us don't have the fortitude of SEALs, we can still take some of their lessons to heart and put them into practice. Emile Hirsch, the actor who portrayed Danny Dietz in the film, said of the SEALs' self-reliance and confidence: "They [the SEALs] see a huge challenge that scares them and that's what interests them." Equally pertinent is a comment made by an actual Navy SEAL who consulted on the film with Luttrell to ensure authenticity: "If you never quit, you'll never know how to."

CHAPTER 8
YOU GOTTA HAVE FAITH

"This poor man called, and the LORD heard him; he saved him out of all his troubles."
—PSALMS 34:6

WHEN I LOOK into the cells at the adult detention center I work at, I often see men reading Bibles or Korans. This isn't unusual; religion is frequently incorporated into jail and prison systems through visitations and by faith-based groups who meet the inmates to try and help them redeem themselves and get their lives back on the right track. It's a legitimate method of rehabilitation, as it stresses a deeper appreciation for and examination of the long-term consequences of one's actions, encourages a more empathetic mindset, a moral compass, and provides those inmates who entered into criminal organizations for want of acceptance a new place to feel like they belong.

Yet despite being provided to inmates in county, state, and federal penal institutions, religion is by-and-large not permitted in public schools, places where children are supposed to obtain an appreciation for the moral foundation of social behavior. Policy changes, such as the elimination of prayer in school, are yet another symptom of the moral degradation the United States has seen over the past fifty years, as a cultural shift towards a more secular society becomes more pronounced.

William Jeynes, a professor at California State College in Long Beach, found there to be a correlation between a lack of behavioral and moral grounding from religion and social consequences, and plummeting academic achievement, an increased rate of out-of-wed-lock births, an increase in illegal drug use and juvenile crime, and a deterioration of student behavior[1].

The need for spiritual fulfillment is just as present in teens as the need for peer approval and acceptance. In the absence of a socially accepted and established religious tradition, teens will instead seek out the darker sides of spirituality, a trend which contributed to the rise of goth and heavy metal subcultures among teens. These belief systems, which prize the individual above the group and the satisfaction of personal desires over the greater good, only serve to exacerbate tendencies toward violent behavior, as a form of strengthening ties to this belief system.

One of the most infamous criminals of the twentieth century followed this path. David Berkowtiz terrorized New York City in the mid-seventies as the "Son of Sam", during which he was responsible for the murder of six young people and the wounding of seven more, until his arrest in August 1977. He was sentenced to six consecutive life sentences.

Initially, Berkowitz told investigators that he killed at the behest of orders he received from his neighbor's demonic dog. He later recanted this confession and said he belonged to a Satanic cult that inspired the killings.

Berkowitz's background is startlingly similar to so many young people who commit violent crimes. "Ever since I was a small child, my life seemed to be filled with torment," he explained. "I would often have seizures in which I would roll on the floor. Sometimes furniture would get knocked over. When these attacks came, it felt as if something was entering me. My mother, who has long since passed away, had no control over me. I was like a wild and destructive animal. My father had to pin me to the floor until these attacks stopped.

"When I was in public school, I was so violent and disruptive that a teacher, who had become so angry at me, grabbed me in a headlock and threw me out of his classroom. I was getting into a lot of fights, too. Eventually I crossed that invisible line of no return. After years of mental torment, behavioral problems, deep inner struggles and my own rebellious ways, I became the criminal that, at the time, it seemed as if it was my destiny to become"[2].

But a metamorphosis occurred in 1987, when Berkowitz was given a Bible by a fellow inmate and read Psalms 34:6, cited at the top of this chapter: "This poor man called, and the LORD heard him; he saved him out of all his troubles." This simple phrase turned Berkowitz around, ultimately leading him to become a born again Christian and launch a prison ministry. Imagine how many lives could have been saved had Berkowitz been given this grounding in personal, uplifting faith at a younger age?

Unfortunately, this sort of faith is seen as unattractive to many teens, who prefer to embrace their affinity towards the darker side of spirituality, sometimes to extreme levels. In 2016, an eighteen-year-old Houston teen was charged with the murder of his sixteen-year-old friend in what was called a satanic ritual. In 2017, two teen members of MS-13 were charged with the ritualistic murder of a fifteen-year-old girl. Ricky Kasso, the infamous Acid King, brutally tortured and murdered his seventeen-year-old friend on Long Island in 1984 in what was also deemed a ritualistic murder.

These incidents are presented here to again demonstrate that teens are possessed of a natural, inherent desire for a spiritual element in their lives. This, taken with the stories of inmates turning to religion as a way to atone for their past actions, reinforces the earlier question of why we seem to think morality is something that can only be found after-the-fact. Berkowitz, like thousands before him and countless more to come, floundered through life looking for something to grasp on to, to help ground them. Granted, many times these behaviors are motivated or compounded by mental illness or substance abuse, which is leading to their more dubious behaviors. Yet in both extremes, these behaviors represent a cry for help—one that we can answer, if we are willing to acknowledge the value that a spiritually aware education and upbringing can have for teenagers.

WARNING SIGNS TO WATCH FOR

There is no shortage of warning signs for parents and educators to look for when their teen is heading down a dark path. The first step is distinguishing between contemporary countercultures (such as "goth" subculture) and what should properly be considered as "Satanic".

Gothic Counterculture

Goth, from the word "gothic," is a counterculture distinguished by its adherents being attracted to things perceived as "dark," but which are not necessarily considered dangerous or satanic by the dominant, or mainstream culture. Goths are typically characterized as being dressed in black clothing from head to toe, usually accessorizing with chains and dark eye liner. Their preferred music loud, with a focus on darker themes like death and suffering.

But there is more at play here than a preference for a darker aesthetic. In an article for Britain's Guardian newspaper, Polly Curtis and John Carvel cited research that studied 1,300 Scottish school teens. Of the twenty-five who identified as goths, fifty-three percent had harmed themselves in the past, and forty-seven percent had committed suicide. "Although only fairly small numbers of young people identify as belonging to the goth subculture, rates of self-harm and attempted suicide are very high. One common suggestion is they may be copying subcultural icons or peers. But since more reported self-harm before, rather than after, becoming a goth, this suggests young people with a tendency to self-harm are attracted to the goth subculture", said researcher Robert Young[3].

Another British study published in 2015 confirmed these findings. Of 5,357 participants who identified as goths, 3,694 reported depression and self-harm outcomes at eighteen years old[4].

The question raised by these reports is, at what point should our permissive attitude towards allowing our children self-expression be put aside, in favor of determining whether what we think is a fad or a phase is actually a cry for help?

Heavy Metal

Comparable to the gothic subculture is the culture surrounding heavy metal music, typified by demonic representation, loud, violent music, and an emphasis on personal empowerment through rebellion. This proves particularly attractive to teens looking for an avenue of direct rebellion against parents who advocate a religious ethos for the family.

Similar to the goth predilection towards self-harm, parents must be aware of the line between self-expression and self-destructive behavior. During the turbulent emotional teenage years, when their brains are not yet fully developed and able to distinguish between what is aesthetic and what is real, cultures of violence like heavy metal can easily set teens down the wrong path. Most people aren't aware of this, but the notorious MS-13 gang actually started as a group of heavy metal fans. The gesture known as "throwing up the horns," holding one's fist up with index and pinkie finger extended, was adopted as an "M," for the first letter of the gang's name.

Again, not all heavy metal fans are dangerous or violent, just as not all heavy metal fans are actively engaged in the demon worship that forms a core part of that subculture's aesthetic. But teens are generally not at a place in their life to successfully build a balance between musical appreciation and personal destruction. Things like alcohol abuse, grotesque tattoos and excessive body piercing are all signs that a teen is not beyond enduring pain to find a place to belong or a (in their mind) meaningful path to self-expression. This speaks to a real need, one which they will try to fill for themselves if we do not provide a healthy alternative.

Teens will always struggle with finding their own identity. The direction they choose may be based on environment, peers, or media; it may be a means to gain attention, or to disguise or distract from depressive tendencies through acceptance in a social group. It is the latter case that parents/educators must keep a close watch on.

FAITH-BASED ORGANIZATIONS

Faith-based organizations have long had a compelling impact on decreasing youth violence. In particular, what strengthens the relationships between teens and FBOs is that these groups are typically non-judgmental. They understand that teens can be led down the wrong path and need adult guidance/mentoring (which may be lacking in the home), educational and recreational resources, as well as a positive prospect for the future. Most of the successful programs in the U.S. utilize peer volunteers who themselves have escaped a violent environment or gang, demonstrating to at-risk teens that it is possible to take an alternative path in life and that their future doesn't have to be predicated on their past.

The efforts of faith-based organizations can be further supported by the communities they work with. There have been amazing results seen in cases of communities mobilizing to speak out against violence, advocating reconciliation to erase any stigma of past behaviors, mentoring with adults, and providing gang-free environments where teens can get together without fear of violence.

One of the most successful faith-based programs is Homeboy Industries, founded in 1988 by Jesuit priest Father Gregory Boyle. Saddened by the increasing number of funerals he was presiding over for murdered young gang members in his California parish, Fr. Boyle mobilized a network of businesses who agreed to hire gang members who saw the futility of that lifestyle. One program led to another, including programs that provide educational and legal services, substance abuse programs, and even tattoo removal. The message of Fr. Boyle was one of hope and giving at-risk teens options: "Gang violence is about a lethal absence of hope," Father Boyle has said. "Nobody has ever met a hopeful kid who joined a gang."[5]

STRATEGIES

Looking at the social and spiritual benefits of having some kind of acceptable faith-based strategy in place to prevent and mitigate violence, a few factors become clear. Regardless of the content of the program, it must be steeped in the principles of love, forgiveness, hope, and tolerance. So much teen violence is caused by a perception of disrespect from others. "Dogging" someone, or defiantly staring them down, has caused more death than we would like to imagine. The principles espoused by a faith-based program, particularly those of tolerance and forgiveness, teach children to look at instances like these from a new perspective. The hope is that by changing their outlook on life, we can keep them from committing a single act that will define the remainder of their lives.

For parents and educators concerned that their child may be going down a destructive path, one which may benefit from a faith-based response, here are some strategies you can employ:

- Watch for changes in clothes, music, friends, and behavior such as aggression and depression.
- Explore available resources to assist in addressing the teen's choice. Most teens roll their eyes and argue when a parent tells

them something. This is why finding a peer or expert to talk with the teen may be the better option.

- For teens engaging in a counter- or subculture: Engage the teen, and have them explain their attraction to their sub-culture. Do they know what it represents and what the personal and legal consequences could be?

- Be patient. If religion has not been a part of the family structure in the past, you may be in for a challenge. However, most of the successful faith-based anti-youth violence programs are non-judgmental and non-evangelical. Their mission comes from within themselves to help others, not to recruit new members.

- Explore legitimate religious options to engage the teen with, ideally as a family.

CONCLUSION

When looking at the potential causes and solutions to teen violence, the value of a faith-based strategy should not be ignored. The basis for much of our legal system was predicated on the dogma of world's major religions, which can still be effectively employed as a means to instill a moral compass in a teen floundering in a sea of chaos.

Our society attempts to rectify negative behavior through reform and correctional strategies, much as we respond to any illness with drugs and medication. In both cases, results are mixed. It is beyond the scope of this book to tackle questions of separation of church and state. However, it should be reiterated that something seems out-of-place when prayer is banned from schools and encouraged in prisons. If there is value in a faith-based lifestyle, if there are positive aspects to having a healthy spiritual foundation, then we should not restrict it only to our criminals, while withholding it from our children.

CHAPTER 9
HELP WANTED:
ROLE MODELS

"As a parent, you will often serve as an inadvertent example to your child. A child will model himself after you in many areas: how you deal with frustration, settle disagreements and cope with not being able to have the things that you want, to name just three."

—Lawrence Balter

WE'D LIKE TO think that parents are the primary role models for their children, but the reality is this is not always the case. In fact, there are many parents who, owing to their negligent behavior, are parents in name only; biologically related, and little else.

Every child needs guidance and a good example to follow, especially if we expect them to grow to be law abiding and productive adults. Yet our society's path of development has had a profoundly negative impact on the institution of dual parenting and family in general over the past fifty years, and we are still reaping today what we sowed in the 1960s.

ROLE MODELS

Role models are those people whom teens hope to emulate because of a specific interest or accomplishments, whether it be sports, entertainment, or academics. Sports figures have long been considered role models because of their on-field accomplishments; Babe Ruth could be considered the first media-fed superstar that young boys hoped to emulate. Fast forward to the 1990s and you have Michael Jordon, then in the new millennium there was Tiger Woods.

But it was Michael Jordon's contemporary, Charles Barkley, who said it most eloquently in a 1993 Nike commercial. He raised eyebrows and adamantly said, "I'm not paid to be a role model. I'm paid to wreak havoc on the basketball court. Parents should be role models!"

Vicarious role models, or role models outside the home, have human failings that are not always evident on the field. Their actions in their chosen field are representative of their accomplishments, and less so their values and integrity—that has more to do with how they act *off* the field. Babe Ruth was notorious for drinking and carousing until early in the morning before games. Michael Jordon had a renowned affinity to gambling. The 1986 World Series Championship New York Mets were plagued by alcohol and cocaine abuse, an addiction which spilled onto the playing field. Tiger Woods' infidelity temporarily sidetracked his career. For the non-athletic teen who is interested in music, the list of creative artists who ultimately died of substance abuse is a mile long—from Prince and Michael Jackson to Kurt Cobain to Jimi Hendrix, drug overdoses and related suicides have depleted that industry's talent pool.

PARENTS

Parents should be a child's indisputable role models. They should be the ones who set the tone for the physical and emotional development of their child. Children are like sponges, especially at younger ages, and will absorb most anything they observe. This is why parents need to be constantly on their toes in setting a good example through love, nurturing, setting boundaries, and demonstrating good behavior.

It works both ways. As I've said, if a parent wants their child to avoid substance abuse, it is incumbent upon themselves to be cognizant of their own habits. They should watch their temper, especially in the face of adversity or when addressing the other spouse. Most importantly, you must be a parent first and friend second. This can be gut wrenching at times but it needs to be done. Behavioral expectations and parameters need to be established and enforced—not always easy.

America is a country starving for role models to guide our youth onto the right path. And while we would prefer our nation's parents to be role models for their children, that hope cannot always be realistic. According to the U.S. Census Bureau, the number of single parent homes (homes without a father) nearly tripled between 1960 and 2016, from eight to twenty-three percent[1]. Sixty-six percent of African-American children, forty-two percent of Latino children, and twenty-four percent white children live in single parent homes[2]. The data in this report doesn't distinguish whether the single parent is the mother or father; however, the research is glaringly clear that the influence of the presence or absence of a father is unquestionable.

Children living in single parent homes with no father show a poverty rate of nearly forty-eight percent, four times the rate for children living in married couples[3]. This in itself can lead to property crime and drug dealing as a means to generate income just to survive, activities which can ultimately lead to violence. One report found that in some neighborhoods, where there is just a one percent absence rate of fathers, the incidence of violent crime triples[4].

Some have gone so far to correlate the absence of a father with a propensity to be a school shooter[5]. In his July 2015 article for *The Federalist*, "Guess what school shooters came from a fatherless home", Peter Hasson looked at some of the most heinous active shooter incidents up to that time and found that the majority were committed by those from dysfunctional and or fatherless homes. Hasson pointed out Dylann Roof, who killed nine in a Charleston, S.C. church in July 2015. His parents were divorced before he was born but briefly reconciled, producing Roof, who then went on to experience a second divorce from his father and the resulting domestic instability. Jeffrey Weise, who killed ten, including himself, and wounded seven at Red Lakes High School, Minnesota, grew up without a father; his parents divorced before he was born.

Absent from Hasson's article is Thomas "TJ" Lane, who killed three and wounded another three at Chardon High School in Ohio on February 27, 2012. His parents had both been charged with domestic violence; his father also was charged with attempted murder. Drugs and alcohol played heavily in the dysfunction as well. Jaylen Fryberg, another school shooter, who killed five and wounded one at Marysville Pitchuk High School in Washington on October 24, 2014, was a unique case: Fryberg's father was ostensibly tied to the carnage. Raymond Fryberg was issued an order of protection for assaulting his female partner (not his legal wife) and issued a one-year probation, during which time he lied on a gun purchase background application. One of those guns would be used by his son to kill classmates and himself. Fryberg was sentenced to two years for his complicity.

We see this type of family dysfunction in countless similar cases. Adam Lanza, the shooter who would kill twenty-eight at Sandy Hook Elementary School in Connecticut, came from a single-parent home. His single mother, Nancy, ironically an educator herself, was fully aware of her son's mental illness, yet still kept weapons in the house in places that Adam had full access to. Nikolas Cruz, who would kill seventeen at Marjory Stoneman Dougal High School in Florida, lost both of his adopted parents before his rampage.

The correlations are hard to ignore when viewed on this macro scale. But if we were to delve into the carnage occurring on the micro level—say, on the streets of Chicago where gang violence has consumed the Windy City—we would likely see parallels of father absenteeism. This is a compelling contributor to violence that has gone greatly unmentioned.

This discussion in no way is intended to impugn the love and guidance the majority of single mothers impart on their children. There are numerous successes in these circumstances, some even in my own family. However, when the cards are stacked against them in terms of unemployment, poverty, low educational achievement, and no support mechanisms, the potential for their children to be involved in crime increases significantly. If a single mother is fortunate enough to be employed, though often more than one job is required to survive in America's high-priced urban areas, the supervision of the child is absent, regardless of their admirable effort to raise their children.

In his 2008 Father's Day address, former President Barack Obama said, "We know the statistics—that children who grow up without a father are five times more likely to live in poverty and commit crime, nine times more likely to drop out of schools and twenty times more likely to end up in prison. They are more likely to have behavioral problems, or run away from home, or become teenage parents themselves. And the foundations of our community are weaker because of it."

There is no doubt that a lack of a father greatly impacts youth violence. What are we to do when society has become so nonchalant about single parenting? Deep down inside, even the most rebellious teen hungers for guidance. But when none is available at home, they take to the streets as the attraction towards gang life increases significantly. They begin to see gangs as a surrogate family, albeit a negative one.

SURROGATE ROLE MODELS

In a perfect world, all children would have two loving parents to steer them on the right path to making sound decisions. Unfortunately, this is not the case and will likely never be on a large enough scale to have an impact on youth violence. Grandparents and relatives can only pick up so much slack. These have served many children well, including in my family. But there are those whose resources are limited, both physically and financially, which reverts the burden back on the single parent with the concurrent risks of the child going astray.

It still comes down to role models. Children need guidance and proper examples, and if parents can't fill the role, someone else needs to fill the void. We have to examine what options are available and what gives children the best chance for avoiding crime and substance abuse.

Big Brothers and Sisters of America have long served children desperate for an adult support mechanism. They recognize the fact that deep down inside, every child is starved for order in their life but when surrounded by chaos they have little recourse other than to replicate negative behavior. Mentors from the BBSA are vetted and trained to address the needs of children, especially within their own demographic. They show children the benefits of avoiding risky behaviors and provide them with a framework to start safely establishing proper lifestyle habits.

Other valuable mentor sources have emerged from the business community as a means of giving back. Believe it or not, some successful people remember the adversities they experienced while making their mark and hope to make the journey a little easier for young people. Sports, business, and entertainment figures have all rolled up their sleeves to set a real-life example for young people in their private lives. One unique and hopefully successful program, The Last Mile, was launched in 2018 by tech moguls Chris Redlitz and Beverly Parenti, who are working with California inmates—mostly young people—to teach them how to code computer programs and eventually be employed in the prison for a reasonable wage and aid in placement after their release[6]. Twenty-year-old inmate Thalia Ruiz said, "I just felt like I had to show them I can get out, I can rehabilitate and be a better person. I'm not gonna get out and keep doing what I was doing 'cause I'm just gonna end up in the same place that I started, and that's not where I want to be."[7]

A strong and effective role model is one who has empathy for the risk factors the teen is experiencing to better demonstrate the potential to overcome them. This includes an intricate knowledge of the culture the teen is confronting, which is why gang members hoping to escape the grips of a gang are better served by turning to a former gang member. Similarly, an adult who was abused as a child can better serve a child who was abused. Contrast this with even a well-intentioned mentor from the suburbs working with inner city youth. Unless they have experienced what the child is going through, they will struggle to make a connection. The goal must always be to show children that they can overcome their obstacles if given the right direction.

BECOMING A ROLE MODEL

There are certain expectations set for successful role models. If, as a parent, you hope to meet these expectations and fulfill your responsibilities towards your children, understand that your guidance needs to be steeped in personal example. "Do as I say, not as I do," never works. Temper your vices if you expect your child to avoid them. If you enjoy smoking marijuana and don't expect your child to follow suit, think again. And while you're at it, think about how important smoking is to you, and whether you should continue or have it stay so obvious to your child. Reduce your alcohol consumption and drink responsibly. Manage any anger issues that may exist. This is perhaps one of the most impactful on children, as unbridled anger in the home can lead to lives of domestic, public, or personal violence.

You cannot and must not solve all of your child's problems. No parent likes to see their child in pain; however, as previously discussed, facing and overcoming adversity is a part of everyone's emotional development. Learn to advise your children in reasonable problem solving and coping processes. This doesn't mean they should be ignored or refused support; your presence is still valuable. But teaching them the value of taking responsibility for themselves will allow your children to develop skills that will strengthen their resolve. Coping skills that help put issues into perspective will alleviate the acute and chronic effects of trauma.

In short: encourage, don't enable. You shouldn't fight all of your child's battles; it's not good for them or for you. Parents will not always be around for their children and eventually they *will* fall. Making sure the child knows how to pick themselves up without your direct intervention is a welcome accomplishment as long as the problem is handled rationally. Failure to cope with adversity can lead to violent reactions for solutions. Avoid reflecting any anger or disappointment if your child is experiencing a crisis. The crisis is about the child, not you. Provide options, guidance, and support—not judgement.

Don't be afraid to say no. There are times when you can't be your child's friend; you will need to be a parent that makes unpopular decisions. Avoid falling into the trap of your child saying, "Well, all the *other* parents let their kids stay out late!" Establish a clear set of rules and be sure your child knows what they are to avoid ambiguity. Responsible parents know that a child's requests will not always be in their best interest.

As they get older you can give them more flexibility to see how they handle it, and see if they can demonstrate the ability to behave responsibly. There must still be limits set, such as a curfew. One thing to remember is that we do not live in a safe world. Regardless of how responsible your child may seem, there are still those out who will commit intentional or accidental harm. I always cautioned my teenage children to watch their driving and not to be out on the roads late at night. Their reply is typical—that they are always safe drivers—but unfortunately, there are always those who aren't, and there's little my children can do against a drunk driver plowing through a red light.

A case in point is the tragedy of Iowa college student Molly Tibbetts, who went for a jog in July 2018 in the sleepy town of Brooklyn, Iowa where crime is virtually non-existent. By all accounts, Molly was a responsible, well-liked student, and yet in doing something as innocent as taking a jog on a summer day, she was abducted and brutally murdered. It is because of tragedies like these that children need to know what they are up against in this world and how they can defend themselves.

By the same token, don't be afraid to apologize. As much as we hate to admit it, parents are not always right. We do make mistakes in judgement and behavior. Use these instances as "teachable moments". Parental guidance is not about ego. Let your child know you perhaps did not make the right decision or behave the way an adult should. This will allow them to see you as human, one who is able to take responsibility for their actions as a parent. Explain why you said or did what you did, what the impact was, and how it could have been done differently, not, "Because I said so!" For some readers, this may be hard to do; it may feel as though you are exposing a weakness the child can later exploit. In fact, what you are doing is demonstrating a strength. This will show your child that you are fallible but willing to make admissions and concessions.

Avoid saying, "I told you so!" This is an arrogant position to take when your child falls. Instead, ask them what lesson they learned and what would they do differently for a better outcome. This instills a sense of ownership and personal responsibility into the child. By criticizing them for their decision/behaviors you are still enabling them by not allowing them to make their own behavioral modifications. It also gives the impression that the parent is relishing in the child's failure because it somehow proved them right. That said, you should still be there for your child to lend moral support or a shoulder to cry on. Don't leave them hanging alone for the sake of "teaching them the tough lessons."

Lastly, don't be ashamed to have your child evaluated for a mental illness. You as the parent should know when something just isn't right with your child.

Signs to look for include:

- Is there a delay in their mental development?
- Are they having academic or behavioral trouble in school?
- Do they spend a lot of time by themselves?
- Do they lash out for unknown reasons?

The list goes on. Mental illness does not go away by itself. It *can*, however, be repressed—thereby developing into a pressure cooker situation. Recall some of the most violent school shooters and the mental illnesses they faced. Once an illness is identified, ensure consistent compliance with the proper course of therapy and prescriptions. You may also want to do some personal behavioral modifications, since your behavior or the nature of your home life can be an underlying cause for a child's issues.

CONCLUSION

Children are in desperate need of role models to guide them on a path to productive adulthood. I want to make it perfectly clear that single parenthood does not automatically condemn a child to violent behavior. It *does* make it more challenging to provide adequate supervision and guidance in the absence of a quality support mechanism, one which also advocates proper behavior. The task is magnified drastically if there is familial dysfunction, substance abuse or mental illness. This is why mentors serve such a valuable purpose in providing positive directional options where none may exist.

Historically, parenting is one of the most difficult jobs known to man. There is nothing easy about it, but the rewards are great—not only for yourself but for your child. Children inherit some of their parents' behavioral traits not through biology but through experience. Parental substance abuse, criminal behavior, neglect and abuse, and domestic violence are all precursors to a dysfunctional childhood, which develops into dysfunctional adulthood. Both as individuals and as a society, we must stand firm against this distorted sense of normalcy, if we expect our child not to grow up violently.

CHAPTER 10
FINDING AN IDENTITY

"I continue to believe that if children are given the necessary tools to succeed, they will succeed beyond their wildest dreams!"
— DAVID VITTER, FORMER U.S. SENATOR

BOREDOM IS A frequent complaint of teens who engage in destructive behaviors. Whether a teen lives on a farm in rural Nebraska or in an apartment in midtown Manhattan, many feel there is nothing for them to do that interests them. Yet oftentimes, it isn't that teens have nothing to do—they just don't have the means or motivation to do it. As we have seen, there is a lack of guidance currently in place to provide teens with healthy, productive options for how to spend their time.

EXTRACURRICULAR ACTIVITIES

We can look at extracurricular activities as a means to distract teens from anti-social behavior, as well as an outlet for creative expression. Through these activities, children gain the kind of validation for their abilities they may or may not get at home or school, as well as the ability to work constructively with others and develop social skills such as cooperation and compromise for a better outcome, all while striving for a specific goal.

Consider the television show *America's Got Talent*. The variety of skills and talents on display in that program is proof of the versatility of the human imagination. Teenage contestants on the show will frequently say that they are regularly bullied at school because of their looks or chosen activity. Yet, despite this inner and public turmoil, they have the courage and drive to perform in front of millions of people.

There are groups that have taken to a particular art form to avoid street violence. The Future Kingz, a dance group started by two brothers in a gang-infested neighborhood in Chicago, is one example. In an interview, the brothers said their mother would do everything she could to keep her sons from going outside—that's how dangerous the area was. Rather than risk being a victim or recruit of the gang culture that surrounded them, they turned to dance and grew to include other youths from the area.

Other options youths have explored lie in the ever-expanding world of digital technology. Dubbed Generation Z, these children have been born between 1994-2010 and are considered the most tech savvy generation so far, according to entrepreneur.com[1]. Teens are constantly discovering that smart phones, laptops, and iPads can be used for much more than endless banal texting. It has even helped foster an entrepreneurial spirit in some, putting them on the right track to success even achieving success at very young ages.

This technology allows teens to explore creative adaptations in sports, entertainment, social justice, and so on. Of course, this all comes with the caveat that they receive guidance and supervision by mentors as to how these opportunities can be used for personal growth.

MY WIFE AND I set a rule for our children: we didn't care what activity they did as long as they did *something* (something positive, of course). This principle ran us ragged for years until they each found their respective niches. Like many suburban families, we ran from ballet, to twirling, to soccer, to softball, basketball, Caribbean drumming, clarinet and flute…you get the idea. Thankfully, by high school all of our kids had settled into their respective activities, which served them well throughout.

Occupying your children with activities that provide them with stability and a creative outlet isn't easy. It takes effort on the parents' part. And of course we were exhausted and consumed with the stress of life, but we knew that if we were to expect our children to avoid the temptation of risky behavior, we needed to be engaged and guide them on the right path.

SPORTS

A typical option presented to young people to avoid destructive behaviors is sports. However, not all parents are athletic or have any interest in sports, yet still feel it to be the only avenue for their child. The same goes for children—not all children have an interest in sports, and therefore should not be forced to participate just for the sake of having something to do. This will have the opposite of the desired effect, treating children like square pegs to be forced into round holes. Not all activities designed for growth and development are good fits for every child.

That being said, playing sports has always been a popular way to avoid the lure of delinquent activities. In the past, many troubled youths would turn to boxing, now mixed martial arts is a popular alternative. MMA fighter Danny Plyler, once a troubled teen, started a program for at-risk youths in his native Kentucky. "People are starting to realize now that you can take a kid who lives in a tough situation, and uses violence as a source of relief, and you can put them in MMA and they grow up to be cops, or Special Forces, or a fire fighter, instead of criminals," Plyler added. "They can channel that energy in a positive; it doesn't have to be negative."[2]

TECHNICAL TRAINING

In this generation of Core Curriculum requirements, one facet of education that has been virtually eliminated is technical trade and job skill training. The fact is, not all students want to go to college or are capable of college level matriculation. This does not diminish their self-worth in the least; our society desperately needs trade-trained young adults. Speaking for myself, I am embarrassed to admit that as a master's level college educated person, my automotive knowledge is limited to putting gas in the tank. I need to turn to a trained mechanic, who typically makes more money than I do, to repair my vehicle.

THIS HAS ALWAYS been the beauty of America—the trades, and how they built this country. One of my grandfathers was a bricklayer who worked on many of New York's skyscrapers during the 1930s and 1940s. My son is a tank mechanic in the U.S. Army, and will likely gain lucrative employment when his enlistment is up. He's always liked working with his hands and while my wife and I always encouraged college, he preferred to take the mechanical route. Initially, and much to our dismay, he opted not to finish college. But this turned out to be a teachable moment for us, one we would come to support. As long as a child finds a constructive direction, encourage them regardless of what your feelings may be. As long as they are happy and productive, that's all that matters. There's nothing worse than being forced into a career path you have no interest in just to appease the vanity of an adult. Like the Montgomery Gentry song goes: "As long as you are working and putting food on the table, that's something to be proud of."

There is a need for trade-oriented training in schools, who also need to reintroduce those automotive and industrial arts requirements which can lead to vocational-level training. While the potential for at-risk students to attend college exists and can provide valuable direction for their futures, many are already involved in some kind of trade—often more out of necessity than choice. Their family may have a vehicle that requires constant repairs and the money is not always there to have it done professionally. At this point, the teen may step in, especially if it is a single-mother household, and fix the vehicle. These teens need to be brought to the next level and shown that they can make a good living from this skill set nurtured out of necessity.

Resources must be made available to put these plans into motion. To give an example: on Long Island, where MS-13 gained a violent enough foothold to draw national attention, Governor Andrew Cuomo pledged $5.5 million to support after-school programs and job-training initiatives in an effort to divert teens from the lure of gang recruiters[3]. "With these investments, New York is sending a message loud and clear that gang activity has no place in our communities," Cuomo said in a news release. "By taking a holistic approach to the task of combatting gangs on Long Island, we can help protect our neighborhoods and provide opportunities to at-risk youth that will break the cycle of gang violence once and for all."[4]

CONCLUSION

Governor Cuomo is correct: a holistic approach is what is needed to address youth violence. Resources are available through schools, organizations such as the Boys and Girls Club, YMCA, and religious organizations. What restricts the impact of these resources on community is a constant challenge for youths: *access*. In order to be successful, children must have access to these resources—open and unrestricted. Many of the most at-risk youth don't have the network at home to participate in these programs. Either the parent(s) are working, consumed with substance abuse, ambivalent to the needs of their child, or are in jail. Transportation to these resources is often one of the biggest obstacles. Schools and even public transportation services should be employed to aid in this effort.

It takes a village, as they say—if we want safe communities, we need to contribute as well. There is always a need for mentors, Good Samaritans who can facilitate car pools for these kids, and the ability to give these teens a chance by looking not at their history, their clothes or tattoos, but rather their desire to change. There is no overstating the positive impact these changes will have on the lives of at-risk teens.

CHAPTER 11
THE HARSH REALITY OF SPECIAL EDUCATION

"Often, when you're growing up, you don't know what's wrong. We don't talk openly enough about mental illness. How do you know—especially today with the incredibly high stress teens are put under during high school—if you have depression or if you have a mental illness or if you have anxiety? You don't know, because you've never seen it."

—KATHERINE LANGFORD

I**T IS AN** unfortunate reality that our jails have become warehouses for the mentally ill. As mental health services languish across the U.S., we see individuals suffering from manic depression, obsessive compulsive disorder, attention deficit disorder-hyperactivity, and post-traumatic stress disorder, many of whom have turned to drugs or alcohol to numb their symptoms, winding up in a cell through circumstances largely outside their control.

One cause of this failure of the mental health system is what is euphemistically called the Pipeline, referring to the way thousands of children in school special education programs, or who should have been in one, are given insufficient preparation for life outside of the protective cocoon of these programs, a path that typically leads them into the criminal justice system.

According to the Center for Prison Reform, at least one in three children (perhaps as high as seventy percent) in the juvenile justice system is reported to be suffering from an emotional or mental disability[1]. The Center goes on to say that students with emotional disabilities are three times more likely to be arrested before leaving high school than other students. "The vast majority of adults in prison suffer from a disability, and many feel the recent spike in prison populations is due in part to deep problems in the education of children with special needs. In addition, nationwide, at least seventy-three percent of youth with emotional disabilities who drop out of school are arrested within five years."[2]

This data is extremely disturbing. For more than forty years, schools have been attempting to implement comprehensive programs for children with special needs to allow them to flourish academically and socially. Yet the data clearly shows that children in special education programs, while receiving services for their school needs, receive little to no education to prepare them for the "real world" outside. The fact is, thousands of these children leave the confines of school without comprehending the consequences of their actions when confronted by the police or a judge, who will rarely take their disability into account for their action.

As a result, jails have become the final resting place for the mentally ill, most of whom had some kind of condition in their youth that led them down a path of crime. In a 2010 report from the Treatment Advocacy Center and the National Sheriffs Association,[3] between 2004–2005 there were three times more people with serious mental illnesses incarcerated than in hospitals. The study addressed an adult population; however, it is worth considering how many of these incarcerated individuals received any preparation for life in society. I see these consequences on a daily basis when observing and talking to the inmates at my jail.

After thirty years of closing psychiatric facilities in the hopes of more mainstream and inclusive treatment, this strategy has been a dismal failure. Every day around the U.S, the mentally ill wander aimlessly along our streets, either being victimized or being the

MY WIFE IS a special physical educator who is intimately involved in the special education program in our local school district. She often tells me about the students she sees, and how ill-prepared they are for the "real world." This is a sad commentary on the thousands of children who have been diagnosed with some kind of emotional or mental illness and the lack of awareness both they and their parents/caregivers have for their futures outside of school. She has seen years of special needs students left vulnerable to criminal behavior by predators who intend to exploit them. She says it is very easy for these students to be led down the wrong path by gang members and drug dealers, who use the students to conduct their criminal activities in an attempt to be shielded from authorities. Worse, the introduction to this lifestyle often comes from the student's own desire for acceptance into the "cool group."

perpetrator of violence. Many of these are young adults who have left their homes and their families, who may have been unable or unwilling to care for them. These individuals are typically off their medications with no life skills, and yet we wonder why we see spikes in criminal behavior.

IEPS AND IDEA

Children with special needs entering into an assistance program will typically have an Individual Education Plan (IEP) drawn up for them, which is a comprehensive roadmap for their academic program and any necessary accommodations to meet the student's needs. These can range from being provided more time to take examinations, having examinations read to them if they have impaired reading abilities, or smaller class sizes.

While the IEP will typically meet the *academic* needs of the child, when it comes to how they should be considered in disciplinary matters, it's another story. When a special needs child commits a violation of school rules, which may include violence or drugs/alcohol in the school setting, they are evaluated based on the Individuals with Disability Act (IDEA). The range of disciplinary action afforded by this act is closely related not so much exclusively to the action itself, but also to the IEP. In most cases, some form of discipline is handed down, but this can range from severe (to the point of expulsion) or a slap on the wrist, in which the child is verbally told not to do the action again.

According to the IDEA, the management of a child's disciplinary action is pretty much left up to the school, albeit with certain rough guidelines. IDEA states that schools may consider each situation on a case-by-case basis when determining if a change of placement is appropriate for a special education child who violates the school's education code[4]. What this essentially means is that one student accused of beating up another student may be suspended, while another who commits the same infraction may only receive detention. This can cause disparities among cases at individual schools as well as within a district, leading to parents "shopping" for schools, even in other states, looking for a clean slate and the most accommodating or lenient rules.

To give an example: my wife had a troubled autistic student who was highly intelligent but whose parents were completely out of the picture. As a result, the student was being raised by his grandmother. On a regular basis, he would manipulate other students to argue and fight to feed his perceived sense of influence over them. He would also argue with teachers that he was justified in his actions, even when he personally fought with other students.

As a result, when he was disciplined through both in and out-of-school suspension for three days, his grandmother questioned the school's professional ability to serve her grandson's needs. Because she would not acknowledge his bad behavior and provide concurrent punishment, she instead transferred him to another school, hoping for a clean slate.

Manifestation Determination

My son-in-law works as a special educator in southern California. When it comes to disciplinary action against students with special needs, he finds that some schools just suspend or expel the student while others ignore it, referring to their disability as the cause and citing the student's protection under their IEP. When a student is suspended up to ten times in a school year, federal law states that schools must have a "manifestation determination" meeting to determine if the suspensions are due to the student's disability. This is a meeting between all those professionals involved in formulating a student's IEP, meant to determine the role a student's disability played in any rule violations.

For example: if a student with Down's syndrome were to come to school with a gun, he would not be expelled because the result of the manifestation determination meeting will state that the student bringing the gun was a result of his disability.

When a student with an IEP is up for expulsion, this is the process:

1. Five-day suspension (the maximum suspension time per educational code).

2. Manifestation meeting (which occurs right away).

3. If the suspension was not a result of the disability, then an Extension of Suspension meeting is held. Parents are informed of their rights in the expulsion process. The student is suspended indefinitely until the expulsion hearing, which can take a week or two.

4.   An expulsion panel consisting of three district administrators hears the case and determines whether the child should be expelled.

Some teachers, said my son-in-law, joke about the manifestation determination meeting being a "get-out-of-jail-free card," but the process is definitely not ignored.

"For example," he tells me, "I had a student that had a history of cutting herself. She was caught smoking in the back corner of campus. When they searched her bag, they found a small pocket knife in her backpack—a small bladed weapon, really made to dig dirt out of your fingernails. She was suspended for five days. During her suspension, we had a Manifestation Determination meeting per federal law. The IEP team, including myself, agreed that her having the object was a result of her disability. Her father had pictures of her cutting history.

"Fast forward eighteen months later, the same student had a buck knife on her with a four-inch blade, purchased at a local liquor store and I am sure the owner did not card her. It was in her purse. She didn't have any intention to use it at school," he said.

"Her Manifestation Determination meeting determined that it was not a result of her disability and she was up for expulsion. She was going to go in the juvenile court system, but at the eleventh hour, after the county reviewed her records, she was placed in a day treatment center at the school district's expense. She could have been referred to the juvenile court schools to relieve the cost, but the right thing to do was to put her in the day treatment program."

So, what can parents of special needs students do? First, parents should—through the IDEA—familiarize their child with the school's code of conduct, along with any necessary modifications through their IEP, and what the consequences of a violation could mean. This should also include a functional behavioral assessment and behavior intervention plan[5]. This is a fair assessment, one that should include the student's disciplinary history, their ability to understand consequences, any expressions of remorse, and support provided to the student prior to the violation of a school code of conduct. The reason these assessments are done on a case-by-case basis is because there can be any number of unique circumstances that need to be considered by school personnel[6].

DISCIPLINE FOR SPECIAL NEEDS STUDENTS

Among the standard options for disciplining special needs students are detention, in-school suspension, out-of-school suspension, and expulsion, all of which carry their own implications not only to the offending student but school and public safety. This can be impacted by the seriousness of the infraction; for instance, the IDEA stipulates that under most state and local laws, school personnel must report certain crimes that occur on school grounds to the appropriate authorities. In addition, where such crimes constitute a violation of the school's code of student conduct, school authorities may use the relevant discipline provisions related to short-term and long-term removals, including seeking a hearing to remove the student to an interim alternative educational placement if maintaining the current placement is substantially likely to result in injury to the child or others.

The disciplinary process currently being used in schools for special needs students does not prepare them for real-world consequences. In fact, some of the policies may even accelerate their introduction into the criminal justice system. Consider suspensions, where a student is kicked out of school for a period of time. To them, this is not a punishment; it is a gift, especially if there is weak parental/adult support to ensure that the punishment becomes a learning experience. And of course, there is no consequence to the school if the punishment proves ineffective; only the student suffers when they are caught by police, officially entering the Pipeline.

Once these children are in the Pipeline, it is incredibly difficult to escape. Data on recidivism, or the recommitment of crime and subsequent arrest, for juveniles is inconsistent among states, but a 1999 study by the New York State Division of Criminal Justice Services found that of 2,763 incarcerated youth offenders forty-two percent had a mental health issue; seventy-eight percent had a behavior problem in school; and ninety-two percent had educational handicaps. Of this, a startling eighty-one percent of males were re-arrested within three years of being released and forty-five percent of females were re-arrested[7]. These recidivism rates reflect the impact of the special needs student's potentially lifelong journey through the criminal justice system, leading to the men I see every day, sitting in their cells in their fifties and sixties, wondering what could have been done differently.

STRATEGIES

Preparing a special needs child for life after school *is* difficult. The criticisms leveled at the IEP and IDEA programs should not overshadow the challenge these individuals present. But while the elimination of the protective cocoon of home and school is daunting, if key lessons aren't embedded early they will be at risk of entering the Pipeline of a life in and out of jail. Not all special needs children will wind up in jail, but we also can't ignore the available data showing the high number of special needs children and those who should have been considered as such, who are now in jail as juveniles and adults. We cannot continue to ignore this predisposition until after it has occurred.

So, what are schools and families to do to prevent this?

We have to look at how the child's disability is perceived, not only in school but even more importantly at home. There are some families who ignore the fact that their child needs special attention, especially if the parents are themselves of diminished mental capacity, which is always an impediment. This puts the onus on schools to identify a child's special needs, discuss the short and long-term implications with the family, and determine what can be done to accommodate the specific needs of the child.

According to my son-in-law, "We (schools) raise the kids that are placed in our programs. They have little support from family at home. We have to offer positive reinforcements to these students and stray away from negative consequences. Negative consequences do not work. If a student has a history of being impulsive and his impulsiveness gets in the way or creates an unsafe environment, we don't suspend or give the student detention. It doesn't work. Instead, we have the student stay in my classroom so he or she can have access to the general education curriculum and to work on strategies to lessen the student's impulsiveness. We slowly place them back in the general education environment while we monitor progress."

Children need to be taught the consequences of their behavior through targeted lessons and direct supervision. Unfortunately, as we have seen, this is not always done at home. This is not intended to be solely punitive in nature; a child should not be taught that the only consequence of negative behavior is negative punishment. Rather, it should be multi-faceted, pragmatic approach to protecting them and others from the consequences of an unmanaged disability.

Another strategy is to surround the child with positive role models and influences as much as possible. Again, this can be problematic, particularly when they return to a potentially dysfunctional home environment. Ongoing life skills and parenting training is another core value to instill in the child.

Whether we like it or not, schools are the vicarious parenting resources for thousands of at-risk children. While there may be no panacea to all problems, the more life skill lessons and resources that a child can be exposed to an have a positive impact on their adult behavioral outcomes.

CONCLUSION

The risk that a special needs student will enter the pipeline to prison is one which compels us to act in their defense, identifying strategies to prevent more children from slipping through the cracks. We know that mental illness often precludes criminal behavior if left untreated or monitored, and in many cases this negligence begins with the schools, who struggle to act within current policy to determine how best to serve a special needs' child's requirements. While there are processes in place, such as through IDEA and the IEP systems, the lingering question is how well these bureaucratic standards impact the child and their school environment. Punishment, if meted out at all, may not serve the child well in the long term. Out of school suspensions and expulsions risk putting a potentially volatile child in an unsupervised realm that leaves them in touch with an unfiltered society. This can increase the risk of them committing a crime such as home burglaries, or abusing drugs and alcohol.

There needs to be a blanket reassessment on how these students are disciplined. For starters, there should only be in-school suspensions, in a set-up where the student can do school work, be closely monitored, and be kept off the streets. And this school work need not be academic in nature; having students help with cleaning the school and other forms of upkeep can be equally valuable, depending on the circumstances.

There also needs to be some kind of discussion held with school counselors as to the long-term implications of the student's negative behavior on their risk of spending the rest of their life in and out of jail. Finally, if an incident gets to the point where expulsion is necessary to protect other students and staff, an alternative setting should be employed to prevent what amounts to the total abandonment of an at-risk child.

CHAPTER 12
JUVENILE JUSTICE

"I think it's important for us as a society to remember that the youth within juvenile justice systems are, most of the time, youths who simply haven't had the right mentors and supporters around them—because of circumstances beyond their control."
—Q'ORIANKA KILCHER

TO SOME, THE term "juvenile justice" may sound like an oxymoron. But when young people commit crimes, there *are* victims, whether due to physical harm or loss/damage to property. The question then becomes: what is the appropriate course of action to hold the perpetrator accountable while attempting to mitigate the potential for reoccurrence of criminal behavior?

This is a highly debated topic: the use of punishment, and to what level, for juvenile versus adult offenders. Debates rage as to the impact a teen's underdeveloped capacity for reasoning and impulsiveness should have on the consideration of their crime, and how it should influence our view on a crime's extent. For example, a teen who is caught stealing a six pack of beer from a convenience store is not prosecuted at the same level as one who murders his family; most will accept that. But how *should* a teen who murders his family be prosecuted? What leniency, if any, should be shown?

In New Mexico in 2013, fifteen-year-old Nehemiah Griego murdered his parents and three siblings, intending to then go on a shooting spree at an Albuquerque area Walmart. According to law enforcement sources at the time, at around 1 AM that fateful morning, Griego allegedly snuck into his parents' bedroom, took out a cache of weapons from the closet, and immediately shot his sleeping mother to death with a .22 rifle. His nine-year-old brother was sleeping next to his mother and was woken by the noise. "So Nehemiah picked up his mother's head to show his brother her bloody face," a report said. "Nehemiah stated his brother became so upset so he shot his brother in the head." He then systematically walked into the room of his crying five and two-year-old sisters and fatally shot them. With the rampage nearly over, Griego waited until his father returned home from working at a church mission at 5 AM and shot him multiple times with an AR-15 rifle[1].

"We never had a case like this, as far as I know, in the state of New Mexico," District Attorney Kari Brandenburg said, "so I can't compare this to any other case"[2].

With no existing precedent in place, the question of how to charge Griego was hotly debated. He was initially charged as an adult, and by 2015 had pled guilty to the murders, when the case took a twist. As part of his plea deal, he was sentenced as a juvenile, and would therefore be released from jail when he turned twenty-one. As an adult, Griego would face over a century in prison. Brandenburg filed an appeal to the court's decision, which is still being played out at the time of this writing.

Determining what should be done with violent youth offenders is often challenging and heart-wrenching, especially to victims and their survivors. But cases like Griego's, while unique in magnitude, are not unique in how they are prosecuted and in what the best outcome for the offender is.

The juvenile justice system attempts to maintain a balance of what is right for the victims as well as the offender. As we have discussed throughout this book, teens are the product of their environment, mental illnesses, and disruptions in what may be perceived as the natural growth process. Most teens don't commit crimes like Griego, but there is an underlying degree of impulsiveness and irrationality that tends to subside as the brain matures. These factors come into play when a court must decide whether to prosecute a youthful offender as a juvenile or adult, and whether jail time is always the best answer. Prison time would seem completely unwarranted in cases of victimless, minor crimes, endangering the child by exposing them to the predatory environment of jail and possible recruitment to higher levels of crime as seen with prison gangs. The core of juvenile justice is not just retribution and punishment, but rather skill development, habilitation, rehabilitation, addressing treatment needs, and successful reintegration of youth into the community[3].

JAILING JUVENILE OFFENDERS

Jailing children is a moral and ethical conundrum. The exposure to predators and more seriously criminally minded youths can accelerate or cement a teen's destiny towards criminal behavior if it isn't addressed early. There is also an increased risk for suicide and trauma.

The preferred considerations when looking at responding to youth crime is to ensure it doesn't happen again. Private and public diversion programs, for example, have shown some promise in not only keeping juveniles from life in a jail cell to showing them there are opportunities that can positively impact their behavior. The core of these programs include education, job and life-skill training, cognitive therapy, counseling that specifically targets the triggers of their adverse behaviors, and recreational activities that build trust and social skills, to name a few.

What is, and most definitely *should* also be included—but is more challenging—is inclusion of the family, not only as a support mechanism but as a way to repair some of the underlying domestic dysfunctions that contributed to the child's behavior in the first place. There may be resistance due to parental denial that there are any problems in their home, embarrassment, lack of family cohesion, and parental dysfunction such as substance abuse or criminal behavior. Despite these obstacles, families can greatly benefit from parenting skill training, counseling for their own addictions/behaviors, learning how to better support the child, and re-establishment of child-parent relationships. If this support mechanism is absent at home, the likelihood the child will be placed in a controlled setting greatly increases.

I have seen it happen many times: vulnerable children are thrown back into the cauldron of their families only to eventually return to the criminal justice system. Determining where to place a youthful offender is dependent on a variety of processes. According to a report conducted for the National Center for Juvenile Justice, this system includes:

Intake

This initial process first screens referred cases. Here, officials will decide what direction to take a case, if at all—the latter of which can be affected by evidence and witnesses. One option explored here is referring the juvenile to a social service agency, probation, paying a fine or making restitution. This is called an "informal" process and appears to be preferred by most prosecutors in lesser incidents to keep juveniles out of jail and to give them a second chance. The formal process deals with more serious crimes and will land the juvenile in court for an adjudicatory or waiver hearing.

Judicial Waiver

Officials here decide whether the case will be prosecuted in juvenile or adult court. If the latter is decided upon, a petition is usually filed in juvenile court asking the juvenile court judge to waive juvenile court jurisdiction over the case, if there is merit to prosecute at the adult level. If the waiver request is denied, the case remains in juvenile court.

Petitioning

If officials decide that a case should be handled formally within the juvenile court, an adjudicatory hearing is scheduled. At the hearing, the juvenile may be determined as being a delinquent or status offender, and the case would then proceed to a disposition hearing. The case can also be dismissed or continued with the caveat the juvenile makes an effort prior to the final decision to pay restitution or attend substance or anger management counseling.

At the disposition hearing, the judge will determine the most appropriate sanction, generally after reviewing a pre-disposition report prepared by a probation department. Depending on the crime, the options include: placement in a youth detention facility where counseling and educational services exist; a group or foster home; probation; in- or out-patient mental health programs; or community service, a fine or restitution. Review hearings are held to monitor the juvenile's progress. Dispositions may be modified as a result.

Of course, there are instances where attempts at compassion fail, through no fault of the involved agencies. Even the best intentions can go awry, and the following case is no exception.

Enrique Palomino was an already troubled 15-year-old when he was implicated in the shooting death of a 60-year-old Albuquerque man. Palomino was not the shooter, but he *was* with a group of other teens who were "mobbing" around the city at the time of the shooting. After pleading guilty to aggravated burglary, conspiracy, larceny and taking a motor vehicle, Palomino was sentenced to a juvenile treatment program, not jail. His compliance was quickly put into question after he was kicked out of two programs following possession of drug paraphernalia and an assault on another youth. Days before he was due to be eligible for supervised probation, he punched another juvenile in the face who "disrespected" him while at the Bernalillo County Juvenile Detention Center. Now eighteen, prosecutors are trying to get him to stay behind bars until he is 21.

IMPROVING THE SYSTEM

The courts and social service agencies are undoubtedly overwhelmed. There have been cases where children have fallen through the cracks with tragic results. If we are to expect more from our children, we must also expect more from the agencies tasked with their well-being.

While the majority of juveniles who commit crimes are arguably not criminals in their own right but are rather direct products of their environments, we cannot afford to be naïve. There *are* some unfortunate cases, though fortunately very few in number, where a child has a pathology or psyche that may not be fixable and allowing them to roam the countryside puts others as well as themselves at risk.

In the extreme are the rare cases where not only are juveniles prosecuted as adults but are actually sentenced to death for their crimes. The eighth amendment to the Constitution serves as the anchor for this debate, with the death sentence being considered cruel and unusual punishment, especially in view of age-related mitigating considerations such as an abusive/neglectful upbringing, mental illness, and undeveloped mental reasoning capabilities.

In 2005, the U.S. Supreme Court voted to outlaw the death penalty for crimes committed by juveniles under the age of eighteen. This decision came in the wake of seventeen men that were executed between 1973-2000 for crimes they committed when they were convicted/sentenced as juveniles, all of whom were seventeen at the time of the crime[4]. In a Supreme Court decision on the juvenile death penalty in the 1980s, Judge Lewis Powell said, "Youth is more than a chronological fact. It is a time of life when a person may be the most susceptible to influence and psychological damage. Our history is replete with laws and judicial recognition that minors, especially in their earlier years, generally are less mature and responsible than adults."[5]

But what, then, is there to do when a Griego or a juvenile school shooter comes through the courts? These individuals, regardless of age, are proverbial ticking time bombs that explode, leaving in their wake death and carnage. There may be an underlying propensity to repeat the violence despite well-intentioned interventions.

It would seem clear that these children will have to be incarcerated. I would argue that this incarceration should be without adults, until they too are adults. The ongoing debate over prison reform must include this discussion. We need to look at age-adjusted incarceration mechanisms to prevent the younger inmates from being preyed upon by older ones. We cannot put a fifteen-year-old triple homicide suspect in the same unit as twenty-five-year-old gangbangers. This is a short and long-term recipe for social disruption.

The reality of these cases is that so long as the juvenile presents a threat to themselves and the public they need to remain incarcerated after they have already committed a violent crime such as murder, rape, carjacking, etc. Fortunately, this is a small minority of youthful offenders.

CONCLUSION

It may be hard to look at many of these offenders with any degree of sympathy, especially given the level of their crime. But as Justice Powell alludes to, we need to look at the root causes of their behaviors. It is hard for a fifteen-year-old to compartmentalize some of the traumas they are exposed to without crossing the threshold from being incorrigible to criminal. All too often, I see offenders who grew up in homes where they didn't know where their next meal was coming from, or where one or both parents are either in jail or strung out on drugs. Consider the struggles of a "normal" teenager and compound those with these challenges. How would we react?

This by no means condones criminal behavior. But how do we fix the problem of juveniles that commit crimes when we struggle as a society to fix what ails the adults?

This remains a noble fight with hopeful expectations. After all, there is nothing worse than a wasted life, especially at such a young age. Juveniles who commit crimes must be held accountable, that's true; and if jail isn't a feasible option, there needs to be a mechanism for restitution. Lawyers may need to step aside and let common sense prevail. If the juvenile doesn't have the resources to pay back their crime, which they usually won't, then let them work it off and use the funds to repay the victim. This will teach them accountability as well as responsible work skills. Counseling, whether for the individual, in a group or as a family, is key for them to learn how to live with and legally adjust to their personal circumstances. The fundamental goal for a juvenile justice program must be to give these teens hope—to provide a sense that what they did was wrong but that there is a full life ahead of them to make amends and be productive.

CHAPTER 13

SETTING BOUNDARIES

"You can make your children safe in the world, or you can try to make a world safe for children."
—Unknown

CHILDREN REQUIRE STRUCTURE in order to grow into functioning adults in society. There may be resistance and rebellion—we all recall those periods from our teen years—but for the most part, deep down inside we welcomed the structure. Providing this structure must be a cooperative effort from parents and guardians, schools, and society at large. Any weak link in this chain can result in widespread juvenile delinquency.

Attempts at guidance, mentoring, and structure are often met with resistance, either from the child or outside influences. Consider the case of a New Jersey teen who sued her parents for child support to pay for her private school tuition. Fortunately, the judge found the very premise of the case absurd, and quickly dismissed it[1]. The father of the teen reports that his rebellious daughter had previously run away from home because she did not want to follow house rules, which included chores and a curfew[2]. Judge Peter Bogaard's decision saved countless parents from similar fates, as establishing any precedent for legally sanctioned teenage rebellion would have been a blow to societal stability as a whole.

Adolescents *need* to have boundaries. What's more, these boundaries need to be established by responsible adults, ideally the parents. Schools and communities must look at establishing strategies that will mitigate public and school acts of violence, and the threat thereof.

These are typically controversial propositions, ones which deal with the tricky issue of adolescent freedom of speech and expression, but are nevertheless necessary, both for the benefit to the teens themselves and to the public.

CURFEWS

Many courts have upheld the legality of teen curfews, citing the benefits afforded by these rules to both the teens themselves (protecting them from victimization) as well as the public. When the actual impact on crime is analyzed (putting aside the hurt feelings of teenagers), the data supports the efficacy of curfew policies. In looking at a possible correlation between curfews and crimes, a 2016 report that looked at FBI juvenile crime data between 1995–2011 found an eleven percent drop in arrests for manslaughter or murder, a five percent drop for larceny, and a four percent drop for aggravated assault[3]. The theory goes that if teens are limited from driving around doing nothing, the potential for violence is decreased. "It seemed intuitive to us that having a curfew on driving hours affected the probability that teenagers would get themselves into trouble," said co-researcher Monica Deza, Assistant Professor for Economics at the University of Texas, Dallas[4].

Deza's study was not unique—other studies support the concept of a curfew. A 2011 UC Berkley study analyzed FBI adolescent crime data after a curfew was imposed between 1985-2002 in fifty-four large cities with populations over 180,000. This long-term study found similar results to Deza's: juvenile arrests dropped fifteen percent in the first year and approximately ten percent in following years[5].

Opponents of programs like these will cry it is a violation of the civil rights of America's youth. In a 2016 article in the Guardian, the policy used in San Diego is referenced when saying,[6] "Parents should know the activities and whereabouts of their minor children (under 18 years old) and make sure that they are home during curfew hours, which is the period from 10 PM any evening of the week until 6 AM the following day in the City of San Diego." Both the minor and parents can be cited, but the majority of offending teens are referred to a diversion program, which has had some promise. Mike Males of the Center on Juvenile and Criminal Justice weighed in in the article by saying, "It's insane. No other country does this." He says that there is no strong evidence that this policy truly mitigates crime. Yet San Diego remains one of the safest cities in the U.S. The point is, curfews *do* work.

The reality of the issue strikes home in the case of two homeless Navajo men who were savagely beaten, one fatally, by three teens in 2014. In 2017, one of the suspects, Gilbert Tafoya, who was fifteen years old at the time of the brutal assault, was sentenced to twenty years in prison for his part in the attack. The trio also admitted to some fifty other assaults of homeless people in Albuquerque in the months leading up to the homicide. During a court hearing for Tafoya, a neuropsychologist testified that Tafoya grew up in an emotionally neglectful home and was not properly supervised by his parents[7]. Having a legally enforced curfew, one which may have forced Tafoya's parents to provide more supervision, could potentially have prevented this tragedy.

SCHOOL UNIFORMS

By early August, we see racks and racks of navy blue and khaki pants and white and blue polo shirts overwhelming departments and discount stores in many communities around the country, intended to service the demand for school uniforms. Many public schools, at least on the elementary level, have now mandated that students wear uniforms. Traditionally the domain of private schools, this practice has garnered increasing popularity in schools since the mid-1990s as a way to mitigate school violence. Like curfews, this change has shown promise in achieving that goal.

Data supporting the efficacy of a school uniform policy dates back to the mid-1990s when Long Beach Unified School District became one of the first schools in the country to implement such a policy. Their ensuing data served as a framework for other districts to follow suit across the country. After two years of a uniform policy in grades K–8, assaults and battery were down thirty-four percent; assaults with a deadly weapon were cut in half; robberies dropped by sixty-five percent; weapons possession dropped by more than half; drug possession was down sixty-nine percent; and vandalism dropped eighteen percent[8].

The majority of objections raised by student and parent opponents of a school dress code center mostly along the lines of subjective sentiments such as a suppression of personal identity and expression. There is nothing wrong with these two developmental traits; everybody needs to explore their personal identities to see where they most comfortably fit. What this line of reasoning ignores, however, is the benefits these polices provide to schools, while opposing them on the grounds of inconvenience. Personal expression can easily be explored during after-school hours.

Among the more prominent benefits of school uniform polices are the following:

Decreases the opportunity for students to "represent" gangs. This is by no means foolproof; the popularity of navy blue clothing allows for students to rep the Crips, Surenos and even MS-13, all of whom have been associated with the color blue. What's more, ongoing efforts are needed to train school officials in the creative ways gang members can manipulate a uniform policy or accessorize to still "represent".

These can be subtle methods, such as hair styles, shoe lace colors, belt colors, even jewelry and religious icons. But, much like curfews, it provides a strong start.

A prohibition on over-sizing uniforms. Uniforms must be worn in correct size. Students and parents may argue they are in compliance with the stated policy when dressed in a uniform that is several sizes too large for them, but the problem with this is that it can increase the potential to conceal weapons.

Uniforms mitigate peer pressure and the potential for bullying. When everyone is required to look the same, it eliminates a real or perceived hierarchal system in the school based on wardrobe.

Assists school officials in identifying individuals that do not belong in the school. Nikolas Cruz is one example of how this policy can benefit officials. While he was expelled from the school, he was initially able to move through the halls like other students until he launched his attack. When he was arrested following his attack, Cruz was wearing a wine-colored ROTC polo shirt, black pants and black boots[9].

Unfortunately, these policies essentially disappear when a student reaches middle and high school, the period in their life when they become the most vulnerable and need this kind of structure. The National Center for Education Statistics reported during the 2015–2016 school year, twenty-five percent of elementary schools required uniforms; however, that number dwindled to twenty percent for middle school and twelve percent for high schools[10]. The resistance to a uniform policy seen in these age groups is potentially overwhelming for school boards, but if we truly want to look at violence mitigation strategies for schools, junior and senior high school dress codes should be adhered to.

The options for those who oppose such policies are to transfer to a school that doesn't have a uniform policy or be home schooled. There needs to be a determination on the part of the administrators to implement this and remember their obligation to students involves their education and safety, not their fashion preferences.

SAFETY ZONES

Safety zones should be established throughout communities so parents and students can have a sense of security as they walk to and from school. The times before and after school are typically when gangs do much of their recruiting and intimidating. Varying levels of security can be established in concentric circles around schools to include school security, local law enforcement, augmented by their reserve or community service units, and businesses who actively want to provide a safe haven for students who feel threatened. These individuals can also be beneficial in observing trends in the community that police may not otherwise be aware of.

With so much uncertainty on the streets of America and police resources being stretched to their limit, communities need to mobilize themselves to be observant of criminal trends and be willing to immediately communicate these to police. Parents must also play a role in maintaining safety zones as they drive to school to pick up their children. There can be rotating parent patrols—sort of like a community watch—where they drive around a predetermined area for a predetermined time to observe for suspicious activities. Of course, none of these resources would be expected to intervene in potentially dangerous situations; but by at least contacting law enforcement, you create an environment in which gangs are less able to pursue their criminal activities. It's always best to prevent an incident than to have to deal with the consequences.

BROKEN WINDOWS

In 1982, George Kelling and James Wilson published an article in *The Atlantic* that, a decade later, would contribute to the revitalization of New York City, transforming it from a crime-ridden metropolis to a vacation destination with a theme park aura. This article, titled "Broken Windows: The police and neighborhood safety", pertains to the implications of how ignoring small civil and even criminal violations could impact a larger public safety picture[11]. The authors found that unattended property that is vandalized once will attract other acts of vandalism. A domino effect will occur causing more vandalism, which will further demonstrate a community malaise. Once this door opens, crime will enter, and it is very difficult to root it out once it sets down.

Kelling and Wilson evolved this theory from the metaphorical to the actual by alluding to the fact that if social disorder is given the opportunity to flourish, it will do so. In the 1980s and early 1990s, New York City panhandlers, subway turnstile jumpers, vandals and corner vehicle window cleaners flourished in areas were crime was rampant. You would be hard-pressed to find a subway car not covered in graffiti. Vacant lots were community trash repositories.

It was the contention of incoming Mayor Rudolph Giuliani and Police Commissioner Bill Bratton that if small crimes were addressed, there would be a concurrent impact on larger crimes. With the Broken Windows theory of Kelling and Wilson serving as the foundation for a change in the policing paradigm from just crime fighting to social order, the NYPD launched a campaign against these minor offenders. Many of the individuals turned up in this changeover were found to have outstanding warrants for similar or more serious crimes. Communities became empowered again and change occurred.

The impact of the Broken Windows Theory on juvenile delinquency and crime is just as compelling. Every town and city has properties that are neglected; teens with "nothing to do" are attracted to these properties and will vandalize them or turn them into "party houses" where very little good occurs. Following the recession of 2008, the number of abandoned foreclosed houses across America exploded, as did the opportunity for teens to exploit this for their illicit motives associated with drug and alcohol use, truancy, burglary, vandalism, and even violence. "The availability of unoccupied housing is an important draw," says Alfred Blumenstein, a criminology professor at Carnegie Melon University. "It gives kids and criminals the same thing. It gets them off the street and away from where people can see what they are up to and gets them out of the weather."[12]

Broken Windows Theory is not just about literal property damage, it is about the figurative association with the potential for criminal behavior to flourish through ignoring the commitment of minor crimes. Throughout this book, we have seen how it is the *totality* of circumstances that can bring a juvenile to the brink of criminal behavior. In its literal sense, impulsive juvenile behavior can lead to temptation towards property damage, among other things.

What this concept of Broken Windows Theory boils down to on a practical level is that municipalities and private property owners must do what they can to avoid access and unruly behavior in abandoned properties, as well as repair and cover up other forms of vandalism.

CONCLUSION

The need to establish and enforce social behavioral expectations is paramount if we expect to stem juvenile crime. Adolescents hunger for structure, albeit with great resistance. This can be overcome if the teen is included in the decision-making framework of a policy, such as school uniforms or curfews. This participation needs to be reasonable and kept within the scope of the proposed strategy, but this can still assist in their buying in to the proposal. Schools and municipalities should all subscribe to the Broken Windows theory and rapidly address those vacant properties which can be magnets for delinquent or criminal behavior.

CHAPTER 14

OUR CHILDREN ARE OUR FUTURE

"Everywhere man blames nature and fate, yet his fate is mostly but the echo of his character and passions, his mistakes and weaknesses."

—DEMOCRITUS

DEMOCRITUS'S WORDS RING true today as they pertain to youth violence. The still-developing brain is a sponge with a string attached to it, being molded and guided by influences created by adults. Their environments and experiential exposures have a profound impact on their behavior. Dysfunctional families foment dysfunctional children, passing on their dysfunction to future generations where there is no spark of outside inspiration or intervention. Poverty, while a monumental obstacle, is not an excuse for criminal behavior, but obligates the necessity to offer options and opportunities for juveniles to avoid those "attractive" shortcuts to wealth that include drug dealing and robbery/burglary. Media influences must be put into proper context by parents, and not used as a vicarious caregiver in their absence.

Internal pathologies such as mental illness or learning disabilities need to be addressed, not ignored. Once again, this is in the hands of the adults, not the juveniles. Most of the times the juvenile doesn't even realize something is wrong, shrugging things off as "just the way they are."

Schools, meanwhile, are placed in the unfortunate position of being responsible not only for education but for social services. This creates great frustration, especially when cases of things like child abuse are missed and the schools and teachers are held accountable. Educators are asked to bear an overwhelming responsibility in an already-difficult job where much-needed lessons of logic, critical thinking, and responsibility are sacrificed for test results to validate the efficacy of a curriculum, and not the true capabilities of a student.

We must strive to return to a culture of social and civil skill development in the face of overwhelming social challenges wrought by constant messaging in the media. Cigarette commercials have given way to prime-time commercials for sex aids. Most television shows and video games have some kind of sexual or violent undertone. This has become "the new normal" for a generation of teens who are programmed to believe these types of behaviors are socially acceptable.

If a community wants to address juvenile crime at the street level, it must address the environmental issues that can cause it. This requires municipalities and citizens to be pro-active rather than reactive after tragedy has struck or crime has gotten out of hand. Adults can't be reluctant to *be* adults when it comes to raising teens. If adults act like children, what can our expectations be for our children? Look at the adults who are in responsible positions and act like juveniles. This includes politicians, sports figures, and entertainers. Teens look at these "successful" people and think if they can act like that in their social position, it only validates their anti-social behavior. There must be structure in their lives with room to grow. The truth is that juveniles hunger for structure and guidance, even if they don't show it. The value of school dress codes, curfews, safe zones and Broken Windows have all been discussed in this book, and while these may appear to be founded on common sense, our society has *redefined* common sense for the sake of individualism.

Rebellion goes part and parcel with this age group, but setting an example shouldn't be perceived as prohibitive. Though many may disagree with the premise, I have no doubt that the individualistic movements of the 1960s and 1970s have had a profoundly negative impact on today's permissiveness. What proponents of this sort of free spirits individuality fail to realize is that even in past generations, teens have flourished in structured environments while still maintaining their individuality. We must learn to question whether individuality is based solely on what you wear or what time you need to be home, or if it is a result of how you act in society.

Lastly, if we hope to prevent youth violence, we as a society need to provide teens with opportunities and resources such as job training to benefit them. Teens need to see that there is hope as they enter the treacherous waters of adulthood. They need to see that whatever is impacting their behavior now can largely be overcome if given the opportunity.

We've discussed what can potentially go horribly wrong with our adolescents. But it must be remembered that those who become violent are only a small percentage of the demographic. This is no consolation to the victims and their families, who may be scarred for life, but the majority of our youth who face adversity are incredibly resilient and are no less deserving of support than those who have committed crimes.

There is no doubt that there has been a cultural shift in the paradigm of acceptable behavior and the various ways this can impact youth, and I am not advocating a puritanical shift in social norms back to the values of the forties and fifties. But I am saying that freedom of speech and expression does need boundaries and anti-social/criminal behavior must have consequences—designed to be educational and therapeutic, and not just punitive. Violent teens must be actually rehabilitated through social programming to a place where they can engage in more socially accepted and productive behavior. This is where communities need to better contribute to the problematic teens in their midst. Remember: it is easier to provide job training and create opportunities than it is to constantly repair vandalism or incarcerate offenders. Treating the cause will always be more efficient and effective in the long run than treating the symptoms. Our moral compass needs to be reset, by parents, guardians and educators. Discussing acceptable and unacceptable behavior and enforcing the boundaries that support them must form the foundation of child-rearing.

If we choose to ignore these basic tenets, we need not look far when violence erupts. "The fault, dear Brutus, is not in our stars, but in ourselves," as Shakespeare's Julius Caesar famously said. We can acknowledge our environment, we can acknowledge our circumstances, but while this may provide explanation it will never serve as an excuse for violent, anti-social behavior. That is, and will always be, a matter of choice.

ACKNOWLEDGEMENTS

I AM GRATEFULLY INDEBTED to my family for supporting not only this project but my attention deficit/hyper-activity fueled endeavors over the years.

That debt obviously begins with Rachael, my wife of more than forty years. She has been not only an anchor of support but an especially staunch critic that has allowed me to grow as a writer and professional. Her experience as an educator, especially with at-risk students over three decades, has contributed significantly to this project.

My adult children: Jessica, Christina, JoAnne, and John, who have all grown into responsible adults and parents. I am so very proud of all of you. And my grandchildren (so far): Sonny, Gordon, Raven, Haley, Nolan, and Giavanna, you bring me smiles every waking minute of the day.

To the staff and management at Hatherleigh Press, especially Andrew Flach, Ryan Kennedy and Ryan Tumambing, for their support of this project, guidance, editing, and production of this book.

And finally, to the parents, guardians, and educators who try daily to keep our youth on the right path. It is a difficult endeavor that goes unnoticed and unappreciated. My admiration goes out to you for fighting the good fight in complete anonymity. God bless you.

ABOUT THE AUTHOR

Joseph Kolb is the Executive Director for the Southwest Gang Information Center, which collects and shares gang-related information with law enforcement agencies, and provides training to schools, the public, and law enforcement officials in gang identification, prevention, and suppression strategies. Joseph is an instructor in the Criminal Justice program at Western New Mexico University and a Master Instructor for the New Mexico Law Enforcement Academy. He has written for *The New York Times*, FoxNews.com, Reuters News Services, Journal for Homeland Security and Counter Terrorism, Homeland Security Today, and Police One.

REFERENCES

INTRODUCTION

1. Wang, Joy, Neighbors in SW Albuquerque wake up to shattered windshields, https://www.kob.com/albuquerque-news/multiple-neighbors-in-sw-albuquerque-wake-up-to-shattered-windshields/4885986/ , April 30, 2018.

2. KRQE, Teen in critical condition after stealing deputy's patrol car, https://www.kob.com/albuquerque-news/multiple-neighbors-in-sw-albuquerque-wake-up-to-shattered-windshields/4885986/ http://www.krqe.com/news/teen-steals-a-san-juan-county-sheriffs-patrol-car/1009325650, Dec. 19, 2-17

3. Mara, Robert Emmet, Baltimore needs schools like St. Mary's Industrial where Babe Ruth honed his skills, Baltimore Post-Examiner, http://baltimorepostexaminer.com/baltimore-needs-schools-like-st-marys-industrial-where-babe-ruth-honed-his-skills/2012/12/10, Dec. 10, 2012

4. Ibid

5. Worley, Will, Woman who planned the murder of most of her family reveals why she did it: Erin Caffey's father narrowly escaped death but still visits his daughter in prison, https://www.independent.co.uk/news/world/americas/erin-caffey-piers-morgan-woman-who-tried-to-murder-her-entire-family-speaks-out-a7012401.html, May 4, 2016

CHAPTER 1

1. Bennett, William et al., Body Count: Moral poverty...and how to win America's war against crime and drugs, Simon and Schuster, 1996.

2. Huff, Darrell, How to lie with statistics, W.W. Norton & Company, New York, London, 1954.

3. Ibid.

4. U.S. Department of Justice Office of Justice Programs, Offending by juvenile: Homicide, https://www.ojjdp.gov/ojstatbb/offenders/qa03105.asp?qaDate=2015

5. U.S. Department of Justice Office of Justice Programs, Offending by juvenile: Homicide by age, https://www.ojjdp.gov/ojstatbb/offenders/qa03104.asp?qaDate=2015

6. U.S. Department of Justice Office of Justice Programs, Office of Juvenile Justice and delinquency Prevention, Offending by juvenile: Homicide by race, https://www.ojjdp.gov/ojstatbb/offenders/qa03101.asp?qaDate=2015

7. MacDonald, Heather, The war on cops, Encounter Books, New York, 2016

8. Caputo, Angela, Homicides in Chicago down, number of children killed the same, The Chicago Reporter, http://www.chicagoreporter.com/homicides-chicago-down-number-children-killed-stays-same/, April 22, 2014.

9. Fowler, Katherine, et. al, Childhood firearm injuries in the United States, Pediatrics, http://pediatrics.aappublications.org/content/early/2017/06/15/peds.2016-3486, June 2017.

10. FBI, Crime in the United States, 2014, https://ucr.fbi.gov/crime-in-the-u.s/2014/crime-in-the-u.s.-2014/tables/table-32

11. FBI, Crime in the United States, 2016, https://ucr.fbi.gov/crime-in-the-u.s/2016/crime-in-the-u.s.-2016/topic-pages/tables/table-20

12. Center for Disease Control and Prevention, National Vital Statistics Reports, Recent Increases in Injury Mortality Among Children and Adolescents Aged 10–19 Years in the United States: 1999–2016, Volume 67, Number 4 https://www.cdc.gov/nchs/data/nvsr/nvsr67/nvsr67_04.pdf, June 1, 2018

13. Equal Justice Initiative, Juvenile Crime rate continues to drop, Equal Justice Initiative, Montgomery, Ala., https://eji.org/news/juvenile-crime-rate-continues-to-drop, 2013.

14. Fox, James Alan, Trends in juvenile violence: A report to the United States Attorney General on current and future rates of juvenile offending, Bureau of Justice Statistics, https://www.bjs.gov/content/pub/pdf/tjvfox2.pdf, 1996.

15. Ibid.

16. Sands, Geneva, et al., Sixteen-year-old boy judge called a 'one-man crime wave' accused of fatally hitting Baltimore County cop with car, ABC News, https://abcnews.go.com/US/16-year-boy-arrested-connection-baltimore-county-cop/story?id=55348159, May 22, 2018.

17. Boroff, David, Three more teens charged with first-degree murder in slaying of Baltimore County police officer Amy Caprio, New York Daily News, http://www.nydailynews.com/news/crime/teens-charged-slaying-maryland-police-officer-article-1.4005102, May 23, 2018.

18. CBS Baltimore, Police: 4 teens charged in Ofc. Amy Caprio's murder, http://baltimore.cbslocal.com/2018/05/22/16-year-old-arrested-death-of-balt-co-officer/, May 22, 2018.

19. Associated Press, 3 more teens charged in death of Maryland police officer, New York Times, https://www.nytimes.com/aponline/2018/05/22/us/ap-us-officer-killed.html, May 22, 2018.

20. Finkelhor, David and Ormrod, Richard, Homicides of children and youth, U.S. Department of Justice Office of Justice Programs, Office of Juvenile Justice and Delinquency Prevention, https://www.ncjrs.gov/pdffiles1/ojjdp/187239.pdf, 2001.

21. Ibid.

22. Hauser, Christine, Chicago reels as 3 children are gunned down in 4 days, New York Times, https://www.nytimes.com/2017/02/15/us/toddler-killed-chicago-murder.html, February 15, 2017.

CHAPTER 2

1. Wright JP, Dietrich KN, Ris MD, Hornung RW, Wessel SD, Lanphear BP, HO M, Rae MN. Association of prenatal and childhood blood lead concentrations with criminal arrests in early adulthood in PLoS Medicine Vol.5, No. 5, e101 2008.

2. Nevin R. Understanding international crime trends: the legacy of preschool lead exposure in Environmental Research, July 2007 104(3): 315-36.

3. Dietrich KN, Ris MD, Succop PA, Berger OG, Bornschein RL. Early exposure to lead and juvenile delinquency in Neurotoxicology and Teratology 2001; 23(6): 511-18.

4. Reyes, Jessica Wolpaw. Environmental Policy as Social Policy? The Impact of Childhood Lead Exposure on Crime in B.E. Journal of Economic Analysis & Policy 2007; Vol. 7: Iss. 1 (Contributions), Article 51.

5. U.S. Department of Justice Office of Justice Programs, Offending by juvenile: Homicide, https://www.ojjdp.gov/ojstatbb/offenders/qa03105.asp?qaDate=2015

6. Needleman, Herbert L., et. al, Bone lead levels in adjudicated delinquents A case control study, Neurotoxicology and Teratology, http://www.biologicaldiversity.org/campaigns/get_the_lead_out/pdfs/health/Needleman_et_al_2002.pdf, Neurotoxicology and Teratology 24 (2002) pages 711 – 717.

7. Wendell AD. Overview and epidemiology of substance abuse in pregnancy. *Clin Obstet Gynecol.* 2013;56(1):91-96.

8. Ackerman JP, Riggins T, Black MM. A review of the effects of prenatal cocaine exposure among school-aged children. *Pediatrics.* 2010;125(3):554-565. doi:10.1542/peds.2009-0637

9. National Institute on Drug Abuse, Prenatal methamphetamine exposure linked to problems, https://www.drugabuse.gov/news-events/nida-notes/2012/12/prenatal-methamphetamine-exposure-linked-problems, December 21, 2012.10. Besharov, Douglas J., The children of crack: A status report, Public Welfare, Winter 1996, p. 33.

10. Merton, Robert, Social theory and social structure, Free Press, New York, 1957

11. Sutherland Edwin H., Principles of criminology, 3rd edition, Lippincott, Pennsylvania, 1939.

12. Shaw, Clifford R., et. al., Delinquency areas, University of Chicago Press, Chicago, 1929.

13. Ibid

14. Felson, Marcus, Crime in everyday life, Pine Forge Press, Thousand Oaks, Calif. 1994.

15. Clinton, Hillary Rodham, It takes a village, Simon and Schuster, New York, 1996.

16. Johnston, Chuck and Moskowitz, Jessica, Boys charged with murder after sandbag from overpass kills man, CNN, https://www.cnn.com/2017/12/27/us/toledo-teens-charged-throwing-sandbag-overpass-trnd/index.html, December 28, 2017.

17. Indianz.com, Teens accused of killing Navajo men in New Mexico, https://www.indianz.com/News/2014/07/21/teens-accused-of-killing-homel.asp, July 21, 2014.

18. Boetel, Ryan, APD: Teens bludgeoned homeless men to death, Albuquerque Journal, https://www.abqjournal.com/432527/teens-arrested-in-deaths-of-homeless-men.html, July 21, 2014.

19. Ibid.

20. Reisen, Matthew, APD: Two teenagers shot homeless man 'for fun', Albuquerque Journal, https://www.abqjournal.com/1160115/apd-2-teens-shot-killed-homeless-man-just-for-fun-in-march.html, April 17, 2018.

21. Ibid.

22. Pickhardt, Carl E., Aspects of adolescent boredom, Psychology Today, https://www.psychologytoday.com/us/blog/surviving-your-childs-adolescence/201208/aspects-adolescent-boredom, August 27, 2012.

23. Ibid.

24. Wittmer, D.S. and Petersen, S.H., The effects of stress and violence on brain development, https://www.education.com/reference/article/effects-stress-violence-brain-development/, July 20, 2010.

25. Silver JM, Yudofsky SC, Anderson KE. Aggressive disorders. Silver JM, McAllister TW, Yudofsky SC, editors. Textbook of Traumatic Brain Injury. 2nd ed. Washington (DC): American Psychiatric Publishing, Inc.; 2005. p. 259-77.

26. Centers for Disease Control and Prevention, Traumatic brain injury: a guide for criminal justice professionals, Brainline: all about brain injury and PTSD, https://www.brainline.org/article/traumatic-brain-injury-guide-criminal-justice-professionals.

27. Langlois, Jean, Breaking the silence: Violence as a cause and consequence of traumatic brain injury, Brainline: Brainline: all about brain injury and PTSD, https://www.brainline.org/article/breaking-silence-violence-cause-and-consequence-traumatic-brain-injury.

28. American Psychological Association, Graham v. Florida and Sullivan v. Florida, http://www.apa.org/about/offices/ogc/amicus/graham.aspx.

29. Bonnie, Richard J. and Scott, Elizabeth S., The teenage brain: Adolescent brain research and the law, Current Directions in Psychological Science, http://journals.sagepub.com/doi/full/10.1177/0963721412471678, April 16, 2013.

30. Astor, Maggie, Teenager in 'Slender Man' stabbing gets 40 years in mental hospital, New York Times, https://www.nytimes.com/2018/02/01/us/slender-man-case-sentencing.html, Feb. 1, 2018.

31. Ibid.

32. Mauney, Matt, Suicide and Antidepressants, Drugwatch, https://www.drugwatch.com/ssri/suicide/, May 29, 2018.

33. Mauney, Matt, SSRI Antidepressants: Types, uses and risks, Drugwatch, https://www.drugwatch.com/ssri/, May 29, 2018.

34. Ibid.

35. Mengucci, Lora, The creation of senseless violence, psychiatric drugs and kids who kill, tysknews.com, http://www.tysknews.com/Depts/Educate/psychiatric_drugs_kids_who_kill.htm.

36. Ibid.

37. Williams, Lawrence, Why kids kill? Prozac and alternatives, Dr. Wong's Essentials Natural Health website, http://www.totalityof-being.com/FramelessPages/Articles/violence.html.

38. Ibid.

39. NBC News.com, No drugs found in Va. Tech gunman's system, http://www.nbcnews.com/id/19361736/ns/us_news-crime_and_courts/t/no-drugs-found-va-tech-gunmans-system/#.Ww7vpfkvywU, June 21, 2007.

40. Child Trends, Data Bank Indicator: Teen homicide, suicide, and firearm deaths, https://www.childtrends.org/indicators/teen-homicide-suicide-and-firearm-deaths,December 2015.

41. ABC 12 News, Lawyer for suspected Texas shooter says there might have been "teacher-on-student" bullying, http://www.abc12.com/content/news/Lawyer-for-suspected-Texas-shooter-says-there-might-have-been-teacher-on-student-bullying-483132061.html, May 19, 2018.

42. 46.Wan, William, et. al., Texas school shooting suspect was nondescript, betraying growing darkness, Chicago Tribune, http://www.chicagotribune.com/news/nationworld/ct-texas-school-shooting-suspect-20180518-story.html, May 18, 2018.

43. Morrill, Hannah, A Maryland teen is dead after her ex-boyfriend shot her at school, Elle magazine, https:// https://www.elle.com/culture/career-politics/a19573394/maryland-school-shooting-domestic-violence/, March 23, 2018.

44. Associated press, Gallup teen gets 15 years for killing estranged girlfriend, https://www.abqjournal.com/news/state/apnotaho2-27-07.htm, February 27, 2007.

45. Winograd, David, 14-year-old girl charged with murder in fatal shooting of Chicago teen, Time Magazine, http://time.com/81126/chicago-teen-murder/, April 29, 2014

46. National Council on Alcoholism and Drug Dependence, Alcohol, Drugs and Crime, https://www.ncadd.org/about-addiction/alcohol-drugs-and-crime

47. U.S. Attorney's Office District of New Mexico, Reehahlio Carroll Sentenced To Forty Years For Murdering Catholic Nun During Commission Of A Burglary On The Navajo Reservation, https://www.justice.gov/usao-nm/pr/reehahlio-carroll-sentenced-forty-years-murdering-catholic-nun-during-commission-burglary, June 28, 2013.

48. Thompson, Dennis, More teens dying with drugs and violence to blame, HealthDay Reporter, https://www.medicinenet.com/script/main/art.asp?articlekey=212711, June 1, 2018.

49. Ibid.

CHAPTER 3

1. U.S. Attorney's Office, Eastern District of New York, MS-13 Gang Members Indicted For 2016 Murders Of Three Brentwood High School Students: 13 Defendants Charged with Seven Murders, Including the 2016 Murders of 15 Year-Old Nisa Mickens, 16 Year-Old Kayla Cuevas and 18 Year-Old Jose Pena, U.S. Department of Justice, https://www.justice.gov/usao-edny/pr/ms-13-gang-members-indicted-2016-murders-three-brentwood-high-school-students, March 2, 2017.

2. Ibid.

3. Cavallier, Andrea and Ford, James, Teen killed while trying to stop friend's kidnapping in Brentwood; second body found in search for friend, WPIX11 News, http://pix11.com/2016/09/14/teenage-girls-body-found-on-road-in-brentwood-police/, September 14, 2016.

4. Rosenthal, A.M. Thirty-eight witnesses: The Kitty Genovese Case, Melville House, Brooklyn, N.Y., 1964

5. Prendergast, Daniel, et. al, Four bodies found in park likely beaten to death by MS-13, relatives say, New York Post, https://nypost.com/2017/04/13/bodies-of-four-badly-beaten-men-found-in-long-island-park/, April 13, 2017.

6. FBI, The MS 13 Threat: A national assessment, https://archives.fbi.gov/archives/news/stories/2008/january/ms13_011408, 2008.

7. News12 Long Island, Kayla Cuevas' mother files $110M lawsuit against Brentwood School District, http://longisland.news12.com/story/37052962/kayla-cuevas-mother-files-110m-lawsuit-against-brentwood-school-district, December 12, 2017.

8. Ibid.

9. Talty, Stephen, The Black Hand: The epic war between a brilliant detective and the deadliest secret society in American history, Houghton Mifflin Harcourt, Boston, 2017.

10. FBI, 2011 National Gang Threat Assessment, https://www.fbi.gov/stats-services/ publications/2011-national-gang-threat-assessment/

11. Cassada, Raychelle, Teen gangsters: How can you protect your teen from gangs, Psychology Today, https://www. psychologytoday.com/us/blog/teen-angst/201010/teen-gangstas, October 11, 2010.

12. National Gang Center, National Youth Gang Survey Analysis, https://www.nationalgangcenter.gov/Survey-Analysis/ Measuring-the-Extent-of-Gang-Problems, 2012.

13. Cassada Ibid.

14. Crime Insider, Teen gangs linked to 40 percent of New York City shootings, Crime Insider, https://www.cbsnews.com/news/ teen-gangs-linked-to-40-percent-of-new-york-city-shootings/, May 1, 2014.

15. Ibid.

16. Bennett, William, et. al, Body Count: Moral poverty…and how to win America's war against crime and drugs, Simon and Schuster, New York, 1996.

17. Crime Insider Ibid.

18. Brown, Joye, Kayla Cuevas's mom tells how MS 13 gang recruits at school, Newsday, https://www. newsday.com/long-island/columnists/joye-brown/

kayla-cuevas-mom-tells-how-ms-13-gang-recruits-at-
school-1.13761633, June 24, 2017.

19. WJLA, 3 Teens charged for attempting to recruit students at
     Va. High school to join MS 13 gang, http://wjla.com/news/
     crime/3-teens-arrested-for-trying-to-recruit-students-at-va-
     high-school-to-join-ms-13-gang, December 8, 2016.

20. NBC, Father, daughter charged with gang recruiting, https://
     www.nbcwashington.com/news/local/Father-Daughter-
     Charged-With-Gang-Recruiting-62845352.html,
     September 30, 2009.

21. Ibid.

22. Langston, Stephanie, Report: Violent fight at Gallatin High
     School was gang-related, WKRN.com, http://www.wkrn.com/
     news/video-violent-fight-at-gallatin-high-school-caught-on-
     tape/1057519454, March 4, 2017.

23. Caroline May, "Whistle blower: Many unaccompanied
     migrant children placed in care of criminals", Breitbart.com,
     November 27, 2015

24. Blitzer, Jonathan, The teens trapped between a gang and the law:
     On Long Island, unaccompanied minors are caught between the
     violence of MS 13 and the fear of deportation, The New Yorker,
     https://www.newyorker.com/magazine/2018/01/01/the-teens-
     trapped-between-a-gang-and-the-law, January 1, 2018.

25. Eltman, Frank, Body count blamed on MS 13 violence grows,
     NBC News 4, https://www.nbcnewyork.com/news/local/
     Body-Count-Blamed-on-MS-13-Violence-Grows-in-NYC-
     Suburbs-Long-Island-Brentwood-Freeport--456870073.html,
     November 11, 2017.

26. Laflin, Nancy, Police name suspected juvenile gang members, KOAT News, http://www.koat.com/article/police-name-suspected-juvenile-gang-members/8125754, November 3, 2016.

27. Brauer, Angela, APD: Juvenile gangs growing more violent, KOAT News, http://www.koat.com/article/apd-juvenile-gangs-growing-more-violent/7666997, January 5, 2017.

28. Howerton, Matt, Three more members of 'Get Hard Crew' charged with man's murder: Juvenile gang responsible for numerous crimes in metro, KOAT News, http://www.koat.com/article/three-more-members-of-get-hard-crew-charged-in-mans-murder/8518387, December 20, 2016.

29. Ibid.

30. Vincent, Isabel, I was an MS 13 gang member- and got out alive, New York Post, https://nypost.com/2017/06/10/i-was-an-ms-13-gang-member-and-got-out-alive/, June 10, 2017.

31. Ibid.

32. U.S. Department of Justice, Office of Justice Programs, Office of Juvenile Justice and Delinquency Prevention, Truancy: First step to a lifetime of problems, OJJDP, https://www.ncjrs.gov/pdffiles/truncy.pdf, October 1996.

33. Jackson, David and Marx, Gary, Prison data, court files show link between school truancy and crime, Chicago Tribune, http://articles.chicagotribune.com/2013-02-19/news/ct-met-prison-truancy-20130219_1_much-school-public-schools-grades, February 19, 2013.

34. Ibid.

35. Ibid.

36. U.S. Department of Justice, 1862. S Visa Eligibility, https://www.justice.gov/usam/criminal-resource-manual-1862-s-visa-program-eligibility

37. Ibid.

38. USCIS, Victims of criminal activity: U non-immigrant status, https://www.uscis.gov/humanitarian/victims-human-trafficking-other-crimes/victims-criminal-activity-u-nonimmigrant-status/victims-criminal-activity-u-nonimmigrant-status

39. Ibid.

CHAPTER 4

1. Encyclopedia Britanica, Columbine High School shootings, https://www.britannica.com/event/Columbine-High-School-shootings.

2. Cullen, Dave, The depressive and psychopath: At last we know why the Columbine killers did it, Slate.com, http://www.slate.com/articles/news_and_politics/assessment/2004/04/the_depressive_and_the_psychopath.html, April 20, 2004.

3. Langman, Peter, Columbine, bullying and the mind of Eric Harris, Psychology Today.com, https://www.psychologytoday.com/us/blog/keeping-kids-safe/200905/columbine-bullying-and-the-mind-eric-harris, May 20, 2009.

4. Santa Maria, Cara, The mind of a mass murderer: Charles Whitman, brain damage, and violence, Huffington Post, https://www.huffingtonpost.com/2012/03/27/mind-murderer_n_1384102.html, March 28, 2012.

5. Cloud, John, Just a routine school shooting: T.J. Solomon's violent rampage seemed to be a cry for help. Was it a signal that Columbine was just the beginning?, CNN.com, http://edition.cnn.com/ALLPOLITICS/time/1999/05/24/school.shooting.html, May 24, 1999.

6. Ibid.

7. Chuck, Elizabeth, Johnson, Alex, and Siemaszko, Parkland Florida, NBC News, https://www.nbcnews.com/news/us-news/police-respond-shooting-parkland-florida-high-school-n848101, February 15, 2018.

8. 8.Anderson, Curt, Student: Nikolas Cruz said 'get out of here' before Parkland school shooting, WPTV News.com, https://www.wptv.com/news/state/student-nikolas-cruz-said-get-out-of-here-before-parkland-school-shooting, June 22, 2018.

9. Wallman, Brittany, McMahon, Paula, et.al. School shooter Nikolas Cruz: A lost and lonely killer, http://www.sun-sentinel.com/local/broward/parkland/florida-school-shooting/fl-florida-school-shooting-nikolas-cruz-life-20180220-story.html, Sun Sentinal, http://www.sun-sentinel.com/local/broward/parkland/florida-school-shooting/fl-florida-school-shooting-nikolas-cruz-life-20180220-story.html, Feb. 24, 2018.

10. Hanna, Jason, Andone, Dakin, et. al. Alleged shooter at Texas high school spared people he liked, court documents say, CNN.com, https://www.cnn.com/2018/05/18/us/texas-school-shooting/index.html, May, 19, 2018.

11. Ibid.

12. Fernandez, Manny, Fausset, Richard, and Bidgood, Jess, In Texas school shooting, 10 dead, 10 hurt and many unsurprised,

NYTimes.com, https://www.nytimes.com/2018/05/18/us/school-shooting-santa-fe-texas.html, May 18, 2018.

13. Ibid.

14. Ibid.

15. Ryan S. Sultan, Christoph U. Correll, Michael Schoenbaum, Marrisa King, John T. Walkup, Mark Olfson. **National Patterns of Commonly Prescribed Psychotropic Medications to Young People**. *Journal of Child and Adolescent Psychopharmacology*, 2018

16. Zito JM, Safer DJ, dosReis S, et al. Psychotropic practice patterns for youth: A 10-year perspective. Arch Pediatr Adolesc Med. 2003;157:17–25

17. Rushton J, Bruckman D, Kelleher K. Primary care referral of children with psychosocial problems. Arch Pediatr Adolesc Med. 2002;156:592–8

18. Cha, Ariana Eunjung, CDC warns that Americans may be overmedicating youngest children with ADHD, Washington Post.com, https://www.washingtonpost.com/news/to-your-health/wp/2016/05/03/cdc-warns-that-americans-may-be-overmedicating-two-to-five-year-olds-with-adhd/?noredirect=on&utm_term=.a01df05cf253, May 3, 2016.

19. Williams, Eni, Ritalin side effects, Rxlist.com, https://www.rxlist.com/ritalin-side-effects-drug-center.htm, Oct. 31, 2017

20. National Institute of Mental Health, Antidepressant medications for children and adolescents: Information for parents and caregivers, https://www.nimh.nih.gov/health/topics/child-and-adolescent-mental-health/

antidepressant-medications-for-children-and-adolescents-
information-for-parents-and-caregivers.shtml

21. Citizens Commission on Human Rights International,
Psychiatric drugs: Create violence and suicides, school shootings, and other acts of senseless violence, https://www.cchrint.
org/pdfs/violence-report.pdf, March 2018

22. Cowan, Allison Leigh, Adam Lanza's mental problems
'completely untreated' before Newtown shootings, report says,
NYtimes.com, https://www.nytimes.com/2014/11/22/nyregion/
before-newtown-shootings-adam-lanzas-mental-problems-
completely-untreated-report-says.html, November 21, 2014.

23. Ibid.

24. Connecticut Office of the Child Advocate, Shooting at Sandy
Hook Elementary School, http://www.ct.gov/oca/lib/oca/
sandyhook11212014.pdf, November 21, 2014.

25. Ibid.

26. KTRK, Dimitrios Pagourtzis' parents sued by family of Santa
Fe High School shooting victim Chris Stone, abc13.com, http://
abc13.com/santa-fe-victims-family-sues-parents-of-dimitrios-
pagourtzis/3518329/, May 25, 2018.

27. KTRK, Dimitrios Pagourtzis' parents sued by second family
of Santa Fe High School shooting victim, abc13.com, http://
abc13.com/second-santa-fe-family-sues-shooting-suspects-
parents/3566531/, June 5, 2018.

28. McLaughlin, Eliott C., and Park, Madison, Social media paints
picture of racist 'professinal school shooter', CNN.com, https://
www.cnn.com/2018/02/14/us/nikolas-cruz-florida-shooting-
suspect/index.html, February 15, 2018.

29. Quinn, Rob, Teacher sues school over 'gunman' who 'killed' her, newser.com, http://www.newser.com/story/205769/teacher-active-shooter-drill-gave-me-ptsd.html, April 22, 2015.

30. Wang, Joy, Santa Fe school district will be first in the country to adopt new anti-intruder tech, KOB.com, https://www.kob.com/new-mexico-news/santa-fe-school-district-will-be-first-in-the-country-to-adopt-new-anti-intruder-tech/4952268/?cat=504, June 15, 2018.

31. Wood, Mike, Why 'Run, Hide,Fight' is flawed, PoliceOne.com, https://www.policeone.com/active-shooter/articles/190621006-Why-Run-Hide-Fight-is-flawed/, June 15, 2016.

32. Callahan, Rick, Teacher hailed as hero for stopping Indiana school shooter, NYPost.com, https://nypost.com/2018/05/26/teacher-who-confronted-indiana-school-shooter-lauded-as-hero/, May 25, 2018.

33. Anapol, Avery, Pa. school district stocks classrooms with rocks to combat school shooters, thehill.com, http://thehill.com/homenews/state-watch/380016-pennsylvania-school-district-supplies-classrooms-with-buckets-of-rocks, March 23, 2018.

34. National School Safety and Security Services, Arming teachers and school staff: Implementation issues present school boards and administrators with significant responsibility and potential liability, http://www.schoolsecurity.org/trends/arming-teachers-and-school-staff/

35. Ibid.

36. ALICE Training Institute, https://www.alicetraining.com/our-program/alice-training/

CHAPTER 5

1. Stanglin, Doug, and Welch, William M., Two girls arrested on bullying charges after suicide, USA Today, https://www.usatoday.com/story/news/nation/2013/10/15/florida-bullying-arrest-lakeland-suicide/2986079/, October 16, 2013.

2. Ibid

3. Ibid.

4. Hinduja S, Patchin JW. Bullying Beyond the Schoolyard: Preventing and Responding to Cyberbullying. Thousand Oaks, CA: Sage Publications; 2009

5. Statista, Percentage of U.S. population who currently uses any social media from 2008-2018, https://www.statista.com/statistics/273476/percentage-of-us-population-with-a-social-network-profile/, 2018.

6. Statista, Reach of leading social media and networking sites used by teenagers and young adults in the United States as of February 2017, https://www.statista.com/statistics/199242/social-media-and-networking-sites-used-by-us-teenagers/, 2017.

7. TeenSafe, Cyberbullying facts and statistics, https://www.teensafe.com/blog/cyber-bullying-facts-and-statistics/, October 4, 2016.

8. Stopbullying.gov, What is bullying?, https://www.stopbullying.gov/what-is-bullying/index.html.

9. Ibid

10. Center for Disease Control, The relationship between bullying and suicide: What we know and what it means to schools, Center for Disease Control, National Center for Injury

Prevention and Control, Division of Violence Prevention, https://www.cdc.gov/violenceprevention/pdf/bullying-suicide-translation-final-a.pdf.

11. Ibid

12. CBS/AP, Cyberbullying pushed Texas teen to commit suicide, family says, CBS/AP, https://www.cbsnews.com/news/cyberbullying-pushed-texas-teen-commit-suicide-family/, December 2, 2015.

13. Russell, Rucks, Family: Cyberbullying led to teen's suicide, KHOU.com, https://www.khou.com/article/news/family-cyberbullying-led-to-teens-suicide/360371459, December 1, 2016.

14. CBS/AP, Texas couple charged in alleged cyberbullying that led to teen's suicide, CBS/AP, https://www.cbsnews.com/news/texas-couple-charged-in-alleged-cyberbullying-that-led-to-teens-suicide/, March 16, 2017.

15. CBS/AP, Cyberbullying mom guilty of lesser charge, CBS/AP, https://www.cbsnews.com/news/cyberbully-mom-guilty-of-lesser-charge/, November 26, 2008.

16. Cyberbullying.org, Bullying laws across America, https://cyberbullying.org/bullying-laws.

17. Gastaldo, Evann, Parents sue school after bullied daughter, 12, kills self, Newser, http://www.newser.com/story/246588/parents-sue-school-over-12-year-old-daughters-suicide.html, August 1, 2017.

18. George, Cindy, Dad hits accused cyberbullies with lawsuit, Houston Chronicile, https://www.chron.com/life/

mom-houston/article/Dad-hits-accused-cyberbullies-with-lawsuit-2077423.php, June 17, 2011.

19. Fox26, Students talk about the moment shots were fired at Santa Fe High School, Fox 26 Houston, http://www.fox26houston.com/news/students-talk-about-the-moment-shots-were-fired-at-santa-fe-high-school#/, May 29, 2018

20. Morris, Ashley, How gang violence can start on social media: Gang members tend to behave on line just like they do offline, Star News, PoliceOne.com, https://www.policeone.com/social-media-for-cops/articles/168457006-How-gang-violence-can-start-on-social-media/, April 3, 2016.

21. Ibid.

22. Dalton, Andrew, Bay area gang members are boasting about homicides on Instagram, sfist.com, http://sfist.com/2014/02/24/gangs_in_richmond_are_boasting_abou.php, February 24, 2014.

23. Dietz, Kevin and Hutchinson, Derick, Detroit gangs using social media to post hit lists that lead to murders, investigators say, clickondetroit.com, https://www.clickondetroit.com/news/defenders/detroit-gangs-using-social-media-to-post-hit-lists-that-lead-to-murders-investigators-say, February 1, 2017

CHAPTER 6

1. Capehart, Jonathan, 'Hands up, don't shoot' was built on a lie, Washington Post.com, https://www.washingtonpost.com/blogs/post-partisan/wp/2015/03/16/lesson-learned-from-the-shooting-of-michael-brown/?utm_term=.04c2bb4f319b, March 16, 2015.

2. WRAL.com, Mangum found guilty in boyfriend's stabbing death, WRAL.com, https://www.wral.com/

mangum-found-guilty-in-boyfriend-s-stabbing-death/13143246/, November 22, 2013.

3. Tomkins, Aimee, The psychological effects of violent media on children, allpsych.com, https://allpsych.com/journal/violentmedia/, December 14, 2003.

4. Ibid.

5. Hammond, Peter, Does glamorizing violence and villains in films inspire copycat crimes?, movieguide.org, https://www.movieguide.org/news-articles/glamorizing-violence-villains-films-inspire-copycat-crimes.html.

6. Science Daily, Violent video games reduce brain response to violence and increase aggressive behavior, study suggests, Sciencedaily.com, https://www.sciencedaily.com/releases/2011/05/110525151059.htm, May 26, 2011.

7. Ibid.

8. Gentile, Douglas, et. al., Mediators and moderators of long-term effects of violent video games on aggressive behavior, JAMAnetwork.com, https://jamanetwork.com/journals/jamapediatrics/fullarticle/1850198, May 2014.

9. Fox, Maggie, Mass killings inspire copycats, study finds, NBCnews.com, https://www.nbcnews.com/health/health-news/yes-mass-killings-inspire-copycats-study-finds-n386141, June 20, 2015.

10. Ibid.

11. Tufekci, Zeynep, The media needs to stop inspiring copycat murders. Here's how, The Atlantic.com, https://www.theatlantic.com/national/archive/2012/12/

the-media-needs-to-stop-inspiring-copycat-murders-heres-how/266439/, December 19, 2012

12. Ibid.

CHAPTER 7

1. Merryman, Ashley, Losing is good for you, nytimes.com, https://www.nytimes.com/2013/09/25/opinion/losing-is-good-for-you.html, September 24, 2013.

2. Ibid.

3. Diller, Vivian, Do we all deserve gold? Setting kids up to fail, psychologytoday.com, https://www.psychologytoday.com/us/blog/face-it/201111/do-we-all-deserve-gold-setting-kids-fail, November 19, 2011

4. Gray, Madison, The affluenza defense: Judge rules rich kid's rich kidness makes him not liable for deadly drunk driving accident, time.com, http://newsfeed.time.com/2013/12/12/the-affluenza-defense-judge-rules-rich-kids-rich-kid-ness-makes-him-not-liable-for-deadly-drunk-driving-accident/, December 12, 2013.

5. World Health Organization, Violence prevention, the evidence-preventing violence by developing life skills in children and adolescents, www.who.int/violence_injury_prevention/violence/life_skills.pdf.

6. Brady, Sonya, et. al., Adaptive coping reduces the impact of community violence exposure on violent behavior among African-American and Latino male adolescents, Journal of Abnormal Psychology, https://www.ncbi.nlm.nih.gov/pmc/articles/PMC3120137/, vol. 36, Issue 1, January 2008, pp. 105-115.

7.   American Psychology Association, Strategies for controlling your anger: keeping anger in check, American Psychology Association, http://www.apa.org/helpcenter/controlling-anger.aspx/

CHAPTER 8

1.   Starr, Penny, Education expert: removing Bible, prayer from public schools has caused decline, CNSNews.com, https://www.cnsnews.com/news/article/penny-starr/education-expert-removing-bible-prayer-public-schools-has-caused-decline, August 15, 2014.

2.   Berkowitz, David, My testimony, Ariseandshine.org, http://www.ariseandshine.org/testimony-translations.html

3.   Curtis, Polly and Carvel, John, Teen goths more prone to suicide, study shows, theguardian.com, https://www.theguardian.com/society/2006/apr/14/socialcare.uknews, April 14, 2006.

4.   Bowers, Lucy, et. al., Risk of depression and self-harm in teenagers identifying with goth subculture: a longitudinal cohort study, The Lancet, vol. 2, Issue 9, September 2015, pages 793-800.

5.   Homeboy Industries, https://www.homeboyindustries.org/life-at-homeboy/history/

CHAPTER 9

1.   U.S. Census Bureau, The majority of children live with two parents, census bureau reports, census.gov, https://www.census.gov//newsroom/press-releases/2016/cb16-192.html, November 17, 2006.

2. Kids Count, Children in single-parent families by race, datacenter.kidscount.org, https://datacenter.kidscount.org/data/ tables/107-children-in-single-parent-families-by#detailed/1/ any/false/870,573,869,36,868,867,133,38,35,18/10,11,9,12,1,185,13/43 2,431. 2016.

3. U.S. Department of Health & Human Services, Information on poverty and income statistics: A summary of 2012 current population survey data.

4. http://aspe.hhs.gov/hsp/12/PovertyAndIncomeEst/ib.cfm, 2012.

5. *Knoester, C., & Hayne, D.A., Community context, social integration into family, and youth violence, Journal of Marriage and Family 67, 2015, 767-780*

6. *Hasson, Peter, Guess which murderers came from a fatherless home, the federalist.com,* http://thefederalist.com/2015/07/14/ guess-which-mass-murderers-came-from-a-fatherless-home/, *July 14, 2015.*

7. Guynn, Jessica and Diskin, Megan Diskin, Why Silicon Valley is teaming up with San Quentin to train young people to code, KHOU.com, /www.khou.com/article/news/nation-now/why-silicon-valley-is-teaming-up-with-san-quentin-to-train-young-people-to-code/465-37c91bf2-9eba-42f7-b0a1-dee1a22152fc, July 30, 2018.

8. Ibid.

CHAPTER 10

1. Schwabel, Dan, Why 'Gen Z' may be more entrepreneurial than 'Gen Y', entrepreneur.com, https://www.entrepreneur.com/ article/231048, February 3, 2014.

2. BluegrassMMA Staff, Danny Plyler is on a mission to help troubled youth, blugrassmma.com, https://www.bluegrassmma. com/2014/08/danny-plyler-mission-help-troubled-youth/, August 11, 2014.

3. Ibid.

4. Eidler, Scott, $5.5M for after-school, job training programs targets MS 13, newsday.com, https://www.newsday.com/news/region-state/gangs-ms-13-funding-1.18544992, May 14, 2018.

CHAPTER 11

1. Center for Prison Reform, Special Education: Pipeline to Prison?, centerforprisonreform.org, https://centerforprisonreform.org/special-education-pipeline-prison/

2. Ibid.

3. Torrey, E. Fuller, Kennard, Aaron, et.al, More mentally ill persons are in jail and prisons than hospitals: A survey of the states, www.treatmentadvocacycenter.org, http://www.treatmentadvocacycenter.org/storage/documents/final_jails_v_hospitals_study.pdf, May 2010.

4. Great Schools Staff, IDEA 2004 Close up: Discipling students with disabilities, www.greatschools.org, https://www.greatschools.org/gk/articles/idea-2004-close-up-disciplining-students-with-disabilities/, May 20, 2015.

5. Ibid.

6. Ibid.

7. Frederick, Bruce, Factors contributing to recidivism among youth placed with the New York State Division for Youth, New

York State Division for Youth, http://www.criminaljustice. ny.gov/crimnet/ojsa/dfy/dfy_research_report.pdf, 1999.

CHAPTER 12

1. James, Michael s and Curry, Colleen, Alleged teen killer Nehemiah Griego's girlfriend cleared in family murders, ABC news.com, https://abcnews.go.com/US/alleged-mexico-family-killer-nehemiah-griegos-girlfriend-tells/story?id=18290148, January 23, 2013.

2. Ibid.

3. Youth.gov, Juvenile justice, https://youth.gov/youth-topics/ juvenile-justice.

4. Coordinating Council on Juvenile Justice and Delinquency Prevention, Juveniles an the death penalty, U.S. Department of Justice Office of Juvenile Justice and Delinquency Prevention, https://www.ncjrs.gov/pdffiles1/ojjdp/184748.pdf, November 2000.

5. Ibid.

CHAPTER 13

1. CBS News, Judge rules against New Jersey teen suing parents for support, CBS News.com, https://www.cbsnews.com/news/nj-teen-sues-parents-claims-they-kicked-her-out/, March 4, 2014.

2. Ibid.

3. UTD New Center, Study finds that driving curfews may curb teenage crime, The University of Texas at Dallas, https://www.

utdallas.edu/news/2016/3/28-31970_Study-Finds-That-Driving-Curfews-May-Curb-Teenage-_story-wide.html, May 28, 2016.

4. Ibid.

5. Kline, Patrick, The impact of juvenile curfew laws on arrests of youths and adults, American Law and Economics Review, Volume 14, Issue 1, April 1, 2012, Pages 44–67.

6. Root, Tik, Life under curfew for American teens: it's insane, no other country does this, TheGuardian.com, https://www. theguardian.com/us-news/2016/may/28/curfew-laws-san-diego, May 28, 2016.

7. Barnitz, Kathy, Teen gets 20 years for killing homeless man, abqjournal.com, https://www.abqjournal.com/1106878/ youngest-convicted-in-homeless-killings-gets-20-years.html, December 14, 2017.

8. M. Sue Stanley, "School Uniforms and Safety," *Education and Urban Society*, Aug. 1996.

9. McMahon, Paula; Hobbs, Stephen; Geggis, Anne; and Travis, Scott, Nikolas Cruz, Troubled suspect had been expelled from Marjory Stoneman Douglas High School, sun.sentinal.com, http://www.sun-sentinel.com/local/broward/parkland/florida-school-shooting/fl-school-shooting-cruz-20180214-story.html#, February 14, 2018.

10. National Center for Education Statistics, Fast facts: school uniforms, https://nces.ed.gov/fastfacts/display.asp?id=50.

11. Kelling, George L. and Wilson, James Q., Broken Windows: The police and neighborhood safety, The Atlantic, March 1982.

12. Goldman, Russell, Kids party in foreclosed homes, leave wake of vandalism, abcmews.com, https://abcnews.go.com/Business/ Economy/story?id=6999539&page=1, March 4, 2009.